THE
SOLUTION
MINDSET

NIR BASHAN

THE SOLUTION MINDSET

MASTERING THE ART OF PROBLEM SOLVING

WILEY

The manufacturer's authorized representative according to the EU General Product Safety Regulation is Wiley-VCH GmbH, Boschstr. 12, 69469 Weinheim, Germany, e-mail: Product_Safety@wiley.com.

For general information on our other products and services or for technical support, please contact our Customer Care Department within the United States at (800) 762-2974, outside the United States at (317) 572-3993 or fax (317) 572-4002.

Wiley also publishes its books in a variety of electronic formats. Some content that appears in print may not be available in electronic formats. For more information about Wiley products, visit our web site at www.wiley.com.

Library of Congress Cataloging-in-Publication Data is Available:

ISBN: 9781394333448 (Cloth)
ISBN: 9781394333455 (ePub)
ISBN: 9781394333462 (ePDF)

Cover Design: Wiley
Cover Images: © kromkrathog/stock.adobe.com, © ValGraphic/stock.adobe.com
Author Photo: Courtesy of the Author
Printed and bound by CPI Group (UK) Ltd, Croydon, CR0 4YY

C9781394333448_171125

For Jacob & Marisa

Contents

Introduction

I have good news: Any problem in the world can be solved. No matter how big the scope or how deep the problem, any problem can be solved. While there are problems that may feel too big or too overwhelming or simply too impossible to fix, there are solutions to every issue humanity has ever been plagued with. I will show you the light and pure joy that can only come by looking at the world with curiosity, never forgetting that each problem we cause ourselves, we can fix ourselves. I have spent a lifetime solving problems that people said were impossible. And I will share with you how to do it, so that you can do it too.

It is time for a book that uses positivity as the benchmark for improvements in everything that we do – at work or away from work – especially now. I could tell from the very first inklings of this idea that I was onto something special with this book. Things have come together at an unprecedented rate. My keynotes on this topic are sold out. Upon submitting the idea for this book, the editors at Wiley jumped all over it immediately. Friends, neighbors, and strangers are reaching out to me on social media, calling, texting, and asking how they can help. The amazing people you will read about in this book have selflessly given time and treasure to contribute. We are in the midst of a great movement of positivity, possibility, and optimism.

And that is exactly what you hold in your hand, are listening to, or reading on your tablet. This book will make you feel much better about yourself and people in general. It will restore your faith in humanity in a world that is often portrayed like it's going mad. Because when most media spotlight the exceptions and the extreme, the worst, and the wicked, we will showcase the good, the optimistic, the hopeful, and the inspirational.

Why? Because there is so much positive in the world that we quite frankly don't ever get to hear about. Especially happening in different companies and careers. And it's not fair that all we hear is the bad stuff. Most media reporting is done on the extreme cases or the fringe piled high with scare tactics that are meant to drive up ad revenue, clicks, and impressions. But we are creating a great disservice to ourselves when we only focus on that end of the spectrum. This book will act as a counterbalance to the airwaves and dataflows teeming with bad news and drive home the message that there are amazing people doing amazing things in this world through enterprise. And you, too, can join their ranks. This book will show you how.

Fusing Creativity and Innovation into a Superpower

Whether your challenge is a global crisis or something that's impacting your business on a more local scale, creativity and innovation fused into a superpower is the most potent tool for unlocking solutions to any challenges. And there are 10 such superpowers outlined in this book.

Creativity offers results. Innovation offers hope. And when we combine the two, we get the best of humanity. When we feel overwhelmed by messages predicting doom and gloom – constant negative conversations about disruption, climate change, political unrest, AI, and more – creativity and innovation, fused into a superpower, provide light. If you look around the world now, there are huge global issues, and every single one could be solved if people could tap into their creative minds.

I will break down how to solve any challenge you face at work with one of the 10 superpowers in this book. I will seek to show you the origin of the hope, optimism, inspiration, and good in many different sectors, businesses, and services so that you too can choose to practice that same hope and inspiration in your everyday life – be it in your business and career or in your world away from work. I will break down each superpower into three actionable steps that you, too, can take to spread light throughout your world. These steps will enable you to act with vigor and passion to uncover solutions tailor-made for your particular challenge and the limitations in your path. And they will show dramatic improvements in your bottom line.

We will dig deep and cut through the negative headlines that permeate our news cycle to see that people out there are overwhelmingly doing good in the world and making a real difference. And most of those people are ordinary people like you and me. And even more so, these folks are doing good through their business, career, product, or service.

Have you heard about the cop that pulled over the mom for speeding, just to find out that she needed car seats for her kids? Instead of writing her tickets, he bought car seats for the family on his own dime?[1] You think these stories are rare? A one-off perhaps? Google it. You will find scores of stories about police officers donating time and money to those in need, often in the course of their everyday work. Or have you heard about kidney donors going under the knife to donate their own perfectly healthy kidneys[2] to strangers they have never met? Healthy people who, for no other reason than to help humanity, give away perfectly good organs to those in need. Don't believe me? Google that too. There are too many stories to single out. They happen each and every day. We just don't hear about them enough – until now. This book will restore your faith in humanity.

I know that may seem a bit soft in a world that is inundated with hard, cold, quantifiable attributes. In our world, something that cannot be measured is viewed as having no value. But I hope to challenge that assumption. As you will see in the pages of this book, people and companies are making a real difference in ways that far exceed simple measurement. Unlike other books that focus on the ills of humanity, this book is a celebration of the collective spirit of humanity, pushing the bounds of our human experience past darkness and into light.

When most people see darkness, I see light. When most people see limitations, I see opportunities. Where most people see barriers, I see a way through.

What's Possible When We Shift Our Mindset

I have learned to see the world as a shift in perspective from what is impossible to what is possible, and you will learn how to see it that way too. It requires a mindset that perhaps you may not be used to, but its value will become evident as you journey through the pages of this book. This shift in mindset allows you to see hope when others see despair, to see opportunity where others see limits, and to see freedom where others see oppression.

We will look at ordinary people doing extraordinary things, ordinary people who believe that they can chart their own course and change history forever. Some of the people you will meet in this book are working on global issues such as coral reef restoration or water purification. Others are working on workplace issues like human resource problems or supply chain challenges. Through storytelling, case studies, and examples from businesses and people across the world, who at first glance seem to have nothing to do with you or your challenges or problems, you will find commonalities that will inspire you in your career and business.

One example of a big, overwhelming problem is the extreme pollution of the world's oceans. Scientists estimate that there are more than 171 trillion pieces of plastic floating in the oceans.[3] Most of us can agree that this level of pollution is one of the biggest problems humanity faces right now. What are we supposed to do about this? Doom and gloom start to take over. Most of us might feel helpless. It feels impossible. The problem seems just too large. But one organization, The Ocean Cleanup, felt hope. They saw what was possible. They had an audacious goal: to clean up 90% of floating ocean plastic pollution.[4]

How are they doing this? With a simple – and ingenious – creative and innovative solution. They've pinpointed key spots in the world's oceans where garbage accumulates. Using a giant mesh net designed to keep marine life safe, they are able to scoop up ocean debris, which is then recycled into high-quality consumer products.[5] The Ocean Cleanup saw a problem that seemed impossible to overcome, and by fusing creativity and innovation into a problem-solving superpower, they've brought hope to the world.

Another example on a smaller scale involves Dutch bicycle manufacturer VanMoof. Their customers loved their bikes, but one out of every four bikes they shipped arrived damaged. The bikes literally arrived broken to eagerly awaiting customers who had been so excited when their package finally arrived. It felt like an impossible problem that was killing their business. But then they had a wildly creative idea: what if they put an image of a TV on the outside of their box? That would signal to shipping vendors that there was something fragile inside – and who wanted to be responsible for breaking someone's TV? The result? Damages from shipping dropped over 80% – all from this one creative solution.[6] They made what seemed impossible possible.

Ten Superpowers Can Change the World

Whether your problem is a global crisis or something that's impacting your business on a smaller scale, creativity and innovation fused into a superpower is the most potent tool for unlocking solutions. And that is what this book is all about – the secrets of 10 superpowers anyone can use to solve pressing problems. The beauty of this is these 10 superpowers have the potential to save humanity on earth and are the very same tools you can use to thrive in your career or business. And I am confident that you will return to them over and over again for the remainder of your life, not only at work but outside of work, too.

Creativity alone cannot solve your problems. Innovation alone cannot either. But something magical happens to humanity as we fuse the two together and turn them into a superpower. What ends up happening is that all unsolvable problems become solvable. And I will teach you how to use these 10 superpowers in the same way the bike manufacturer or the ocean plastic clean-up organization did. It's amazing what we can do when we harness the power of human ingenuity to solve issues that seem impossible. Even better, I can show you how to solve any business or career challenge using proven superpower techniques – refined over years – now distilled into a list of 10 actionable, repeatable methods for success.

While this may seem like a bold statement, I have seen these 10 superpowers work for global issues and workplace issues alike. My job as a researcher, writer, keynote speaker, and small business owner comes with a unique ability to work across many different industries. That ability to see what is going on in manufacturing, the real estate business, the financial sector, healthcare, aviation, and many other industries has given me the ability to test, retest, tweak, and solidify these 10 superpowers over countless years. These are techniques I have isolated that work across all disciplines, not narrowed for one particular trade, business, product, or service. The universality of the 10 superpowers is exactly what makes them so powerful.

Not only have I worked across a dizzying array of sectors, I have also worked with employees from the front line all the way to the C-suite. I have worked with and presented keynotes to CEOs in the insurance services sector and to manufacturing folks in the steel pipe industry; and while their issues are very different, their resolve to overcome them is the same. And no matter what industry or level of the staff I interact with, I see common questions like:

- How do we find top-tier talent to hire?
- How do I, as an employee, make a difference?
- How do we improve communication across the organization?
- How do we keep up with the ever-evolving cybersecurity needs?
- How do we balance our need for growth while maintaining quality?
- How do we best manage customer/employee expectations?

And in each case, I have applied the 10 superpowers to not only alleviate these concerns but to solve them once and for all. These common challenges, at first glance, seem insurmountable (and many of them became staff roadblocks), but through the practice of using the 10 superpowers, they become attainable goals that hold a deep personal meaning to those setting them.

Our DNA and Problem-Solving

One of the best things about the 10 superpowers is that they are innate to every human being on earth. These superpowers are found in our DNA as humans – they are part and parcel of who we are. This book will help reawaken these long-dormant problem-solving techniques that wait for human beings to awaken them in all their glory and apply them to challenges large and small. The way that each individual uses these 10 superpowers is unique. No two people will ever practice the 10 superpowers in the same way. Over the course of this book, you will find answers to your unique challenges at work, in your community, and beyond.

Each chapter highlights three items you can immediately apply at work because it's not enough to identify the superpower; you need to activate it with actionable, concrete tools. I will show you the "how" of applying a particular superpower in your work environment, no matter what you do.

While this book relies on research to underscore its substance, in reality it's more of a field manual. I did the hard work for you, and now you can apply the lessons learned. A quick note for the naysayers out there: The evidence is overwhelmingly in favor of humanity being able to solve problems that we have gotten ourselves into – and I hope this book will serve as confirmation of the lessons I have gathered over my career, continually solving problems that people thought were impossible.

A Closer Look at Each Superpower

It's amazing what we can do when we harness the power of human ingenuity to solve challenges that seem impossible. And the even better news is that I can show you how to solve any problem or issue that may arise in your business or in your career using battle-hardened techniques that have taken many years, iterations, and evolutions to mature into an actionable and repeatable method of success. These superpowers aren't only for solving granular issues, they also work across many different challenges that we find ourselves in today and give us hope, action, and bold assurance that, yes, indeed, we can take on anything and thrive. This book dedicates one chapter to each superpower.

Superpower #1: Just Start

What Saving Coral Reefs Teaches Us About Taking the Plunge

We will start with a look at the amazing story of CEO Titouan Bernicot who runs a company called Coral Gardeners and how he used the Just Start superpower to become one of the world's foremost experts in coral reef restoration without having spent a day in a marine biology class. It turns out that sometimes Just Start can be one of the best things you can do for your career or business.

Then, we will look at roadblocks that prevent us from Just Starting, especially roadblocks that we deliberately put in front of ourselves to limit our own potential. Why do we do that? And how can we overcome that human tendency to self-sabotage? Next, we look at the value that Just Start can bring us as a transformational method, from mere concept to fully realized execution. And finally, we will feature three incredible takeaway tools that show you how to use the Just Start superpower:

- Your Week of Ideas
- Imagine the Worst
- Own the Transition

Superpower #2: Invest in Yourself

What Renewable Forests and Bourbon Teach Us About the Long Term in a Short-Term World

In this chapter, we will look at the story of a company that is literally changing the landscape of the paper goods industry and a company in the bourbon alcoholic spirits industry doing the same. You might think these companies would be the last on earth to ever think about long-term issues, but they are using the Invest in Yourself superpower in unique and ingenious ways that will inspire you to reinvent how you define Investing in Yourself, literally and figuratively.

Then, we will look at the sheer power of what happens when we invest in ourselves. At first this superpower may seem straightforward, but investing in ourselves can be one of the most powerful milestones we have in our career trajectory to enable amazing progress.

Finally, in this chapter we will look at three takeaways from Invest in Yourself and define our own investment in ourselves to maximize the return in our careers and businesses, no matter what it is we would like to accomplish. We will learn how to implement tools such as:

- Start on the Five
- Take That Class Already
- Make Time for *Your* Big Idea

Superpower #3: Use a Filter

What Life-Saving Innovations for Cleaning Dirty Water Teach Us About Unblocking Our Creative Thinking

In this chapter, we will look at the incredible origin of a company called LifeStraw. They produce and distribute a product that looks like a big plastic straw. It has a powerful passive filter that cleans up to 99.999% of all waterborne bacteria so that people with contaminated water sources can drink clean water. It's a game changer. The images of people using the straw across the world in situations that are less than ideal are simply stunning. And it is saving lives.

Then, we will look at filters and their use in business. And while our own situations aren't usually a matter of life and death, many of us need that same game changer in our lives – a filter to clean up our interactions, our reactions, sometimes even our careers. By purposefully inserting filters (some real and some metaphorical) into our work processes, we introduce milestones that force us to rethink how we approach a problem or challenge us to stop doing the same thing that isn't working over and over again.

Finally, we uncover three Use a Filter tools that can bring incredible benefits to a world that is often moving at breakneck speed. We can also use these tools when we want to block out the noise and distractions that prevent us from tapping into our creative minds. The takeaways from this chapter are:

- Send It Later
- Make More Time
- Don't Make Friends at Work

Superpower #4: Take a Chance

What Re-Imagining Schools in Seychelles Teaches Us About Succeeding When the Odds Seem Insurmountable

In this chapter, we will look at the incredible school system in Seychelles. Most people would be at a loss to even point out Seychelles on a map, much less pronounce it. (It's pronounced: SAY SHELLZ.) It's a small archipelago country consisting of 115 islands in the Indian Ocean, off the coast of East Africa. Something extraordinary is happening there. The school system has been reinvented by Taking a Chance on celebrating its small incremental successes and learning from its failures. It is now the number one public school system in Africa. There have been many failures along the way to success, but educators, civic leaders, and organizers Take a Chance at every opportunity, and the results are striking.

We then look at our own careers and businesses and ask what would happen if we would just Take a Chance instead of dwelling on our failures or inabilities. We see that some of the most creative solutions come from focusing on what we learn through even the smallest kernel of success and how we discover a positive path through our failures. Because sometimes failures are the greatest opportunities to learn.

Finally, we discover three actionable items we can use at work today to help us take advantage of our mistakes and learn to turn adversity into, thereby Taking a Chance on ideas, initiatives, and plans for success. The three takeaways are:

- Fail on Purpose
- Give 'Em a Chance
- Recognize Mistakes and Then Success

Superpower #5: Untangle Complexity

What Health Insurance in Japan Teaches Us About Solving Problems with Simplicity

This superpower teaches us to take away, not add. In this case, what we're taking away is the astonishing human ability to over-complicate things that should be simple! Too many meetings that go nowhere, feeling like you're chasing your tail at work, endlessly bringing up the same thing over and over again? This chapter is for you! Especially when we work someplace where we see, firsthand, people overcomplicating things only to benefit themselves and the bureaucracy. Japan has done a great job in recent years at attempting to curb bureaucracy in their health-care, and they are doing it in a unique way that Untangles Complexity and levels the playing field. Finally, we discover three items we can implement both to help Untangle Complexity in our day-to-day work lives and to face antiquated practices that can no longer keep up with today's rapid changes. The three takeaways tools from this chapter are:

- Edit, Edit, Edit Till You Drop
- End the Tyranny of Endless Decisions
- The Silo Killer

Superpower #6: Look on the Positive Side

What Hiring People with Disabilities Teaches Us About Hidden Treasures

Hiring people is one of the most difficult parts of a business. In all the keynotes I have delivered, especially over the last two years, one thing that comes up regularly in our post-pandemic world is the difficulty of finding people to hire. And after finding people with the right skills, it is challenging to train them, equip them for success, and generate a culture where that success can be replicated across different departments and sectors of the business. My friend Gil Winch has found one way to solve this incredible challenge with his company Call Yachol (CY). We will study his seemingly controversial methods to uncover some amazing creative and innovative fusions that anyone can use. Then, finally, we will look at three takeaways that really work in the field, enabling flexibility, utility, and a sense of adaptability to solve some of your toughest challenges. The three tools we will study in this chapter are:

- Use Better Words
- Newton's Third Law
- Add a Dose of Humanity

Superpower #7: Embrace the Routine

What Civil War Reenactments Teach Us About Thinking Inside the Box

Sometimes the most incredible thing we can do to boost creativity and innovation is to think inside the box, not outside. That may seem counterintuitive because you may have been told to do the opposite your whole life, but it is true. The more we define our box and understand it, the better we are at innovating and creating new and unique problem-solving capabilities. We have to learn the rules before we break them. One unlikely yet completely reasonable way to boost our ability to solve problems is using the superpower of Embracing the Routine. We will look at Civil War reenactors who come out in droves each year to recreate a certain historical battle, keeping every single detail intact. If, in the original battle, there were sixteen cannons in the ridge by the patch of trees, there will be sixteen cannons there in the reenactment. If the Rebels came in from the east by fording the river, reenactors will do that in that same exact spot. This particular attention to detail ensures history does not get corrupted. In a world where any demagogue shouts out from the rooftops their corruption of truth, the truth gets degraded. These reenactors preserve truth by Embracing the Routine. Finally, we will learn three takeaways from embracing routine and honoring truth that we can use right now in our day-to-day lives.

- Evolution, Not Revolution
- Define the Box
- Learn the Rules Before You Break Them

Superpower #8: Fail Successfully

What Prison Reform in Norway Teaches Us About the Power of Making Mistakes

The great Russian novelist Fyodor Dostoevsky once said, "A society should be judged not by how it treats its outstanding citizens but by how it treats its criminals." We're doing a pretty bad job in the United States with how we treat our prisoners, and by extension, with our criminal rehabilitation. My research on the superpower of Failing Successfully takes me to David Lee Windecher in Miami, who, against all odds, harnessed the power of making mistakes into a successful career path. Then, I went all the way to Norway to study its prisons and what the country is doing to rehabilitate prisoners who have made some serious mistakes and are now on the path of redemption. Norway has implemented some amazing systems to help reintegrate offenders back into mainstream society. And while our mistakes don't land us in prison (hopefully), we can still learn a lot from the systems that Norway puts in place to help prisoners Fail Successfully, and implement that in our own careers and businesses. Because let's face it: we all make mistakes, but there is hope. It turns out there is a better way to make mistakes and a better way to fail, and that superpower is what we will uncover in Chapter 8. Doing so can make all the difference between a huge win or a crushing defeat. The tools we will uncover for instant use at work and beyond from this superpower are:

- Live Without Regrets
- Fail Fast and Fail Often
- Slow Overnight Success

Superpower #9: Question the Data

What Global Population Growth Teaches Us About Understanding Metrics

We hear the dire news all the time about humans overpopulating our world. To horrific and deadly extremes. We see images of pollution and overcrowded cities filled with a mass of humanity and we are led to believe that, yes, indeed, overpopulation is a problem! Our first instinct is to get down about it and sulk and hate ourselves for even being born. But is it indeed true? Are we overpopulating like crazy? It turns out that overpopulation is not true. Moreover, the world is experiencing a slowdown in the human birth rate.

So how do we get from the world being overpopulated in our lifetime to a slow decline of the earth's population? By using my next problem-solving superpower: Question the Data. When we're constantly being bombarded by so much conflicting information, being able to Question the Data allows you to examine the stats in a way that brings honesty to light. This chapter will uncover ways for you to Question the Data in your career or business and beyond. And the three techniques that you can use right away to amplify this superpower are:

- You Need More Than Likes: The Gut Check
- Beware the Demagogues
- Seek Balance

Superpower #10: There's No Comparison

What the Things We Tell Ourselves Teach Us About Our Own Unique Problem-Solving Superpowers

Therapists around the world will tell us that we are so dang unhappy all the time because we continually compare ourselves to others. No matter who we compare ourselves to, we seem to always find someone doing way better than us. Better job, better car, better kids, better house, the list goes on and on forever. Social media has shifted this need to compare ourselves with others into hyperdrive. On social media, we are exposed to video after video depicting how great everyone's life is, and we perceive everyone as doing much better than us. Their meals look like Michelin-star meals, their houses are so clean, and their honor-roll kids seem so happy!

It's easy to spiral when we are exposed to social media, but this ruins our ability to solve problems creativily. What we need when fusing together creativity and innovation is the final super-power so we can express our individuality. There is truly no comparison, which in this day and age has become ever more important in the pursuit of happiness and prosperity. We will look at how important our individual DNA is in implementing the 10 superpowers, and we will take away three great tools we can use to grow:

- A Positive Spin
- You as No One Else
- Make Something from Nothing

Your Story Starts Now

It is my sincere hope that this book brings you a ton of comfort and peace in a world that has seemingly gone out of control. It will give you hope and inspiration to try and tackle the many challenges that lie before us because all of those challenges are indeed solvable. In these pages, you will meet some amazing people who are expressing their superpowers everyday.

But this book isn't about them. It's about you.

You have to believe. We have to have faith in our own ability to get us out of whatever jam we have gotten ourselves into. And the good news is that we can indeed do it and we will do it together. These superpowers are life-affirming skills that we can call upon at anytime to get us out of even the stickiest situations.

The stories of people healing what's broken are breathtaking because they show that real transformation is within reach for everyone reading.

At the end of the day, each and every human being on earth has the potential to unlock so many solutions to an equal number of problems that face humanity. And you too may join their ranks, finding the inspiration to solve problems big and small and make the world a better place for all of us.

It all starts with a turn of the page.

Superpower #1: Just Start
What Saving Coral Reefs Teaches Us About Taking the Plunge

Changing the world can be really hard, but it can all start by fixing one broken coral.

—Titouan Bernicot

You will travel to the four corners of the globe with this book, and this first chapter is no exception. Our story begins on a French Polynesian island called Mo'orea, which is a tiny island just off Tahiti. If you can imagine the island Eden paradise of your wildest daydreams, then this is it. Palm trees, beaches, white sand, and crystal-clear waters beckon tourists from around the world to see untouched nature in its glorious God-given best.

I connected with Titouan Bernicot, who is the CEO of a company called Coral Gardeners. He grew up on his family's pearl farm. Far from feeling lonely, he spent most of his time in the sea, catching fish to eat from the reefs and swimming among sealife of all kinds of colors, stripes, and spots. He spent time with his father's staff watching them polish pearls until they shone with brilliance, making a living off the sea. The memories of swimming and exploring the pristine ocean would remain with him for the rest of his life.

It was sometime around his 16th birthday[1] when he and his friends finally managed to save enough money to buy a small boat. They relished their newfound freedom and took the boat out to a favorite surfing spot. It was then that Titouan noticed something peculiar. And what he noticed would set in motion something he would dedicate the rest of his life to preserving.

That fateful day, he noticed that the reef below him looked odd. He jumped in to investigate the normally colorful corals and saw that indeed they had lost their color and turned a pale chalky white. He touched the reef and it crumbled to dust in his hand. He was shocked. Upon returning back home he did what any of us would do – he started to google. He learned quickly from the internet that corals were turning white – what scientists called bleaching – due to rising sea temperatures. He made the decision there and then that he would spend the rest of his life defending and protecting this precious natural resource that is vital for life on earth. He figured that he would be greeted with open arms and embraced for his youthful enthusiasm as the world would welcome a great and wonderful company filled with idealism and drive!

Well, not so fast.

He rushed to meet scientists to tell them his ideas, goals, and dreams of saving reefs. He literally knocked on the doors of whomever would have him at the University of California's Gump Station research lab, which happened to be on Mo'orea. He would tell scientists there, "Guys, I'm sixteen years old, I fell in love with the coral reef, and I want to dedicate my life to helping it. What can I do?"[2]

They looked at him and pretty much scoffed. They would tell him that it was complicated. It was not easy. It was daunting. Plus, he was only 16. They said to him, "Little buddy, calm down. You're only sixteen. You need to finish high school, then study marine biology. If you're smart enough, you can do an eight-year PhD program and then sit at the table with us."

Titouan Bernicot made a decision that would equal his dedication to saving reefs. Because, like most of us, he could have given up. He could have listened to the naysayers and given into their knowledge, their prestige, their elevated lot in life. They were scientists from esteemed institutions known worldwide for marine biology excellence! He was just an ocean kid, a surfer, a diver! But it was then and there that Titouan made the fateful decision to Just Start, which is the superpower that we will cover in this chapter. It is the first superpower on my list for a reason. Nothing happens with your dreams, your ideas, your aspirations, or even your problem-solving skills until you declare once and for all that you will Just Start.

Titouan remembers telling the scientists that he met with when he was a teenager shortly after touching that bleached reef, "You're fucking crazy. I really respect you, and I love science, but I am not going to wait all those years." He told them that one day they will end up working for him and that he needed to Just Start now – helping and doing all he could right away. There was no time to lose. So he did exactly that. And today, his company Coral Gardeners is the most well-respected and largest coral restoration company anywhere in the world. Currently they have coral nurseries in Fiji, Thailand, and Puerto Rico with a full-time staff of over 50 people, some of whom are very much like the marine biologists he met with as a kid. All this good in the world emerged simply because he Just Started and did what he believed would chart his destiny and contribute to the world's improvement.

The Media

Never heard of Titouan Bernicot or his company Coral Gardeners until you read about him in this book? That's not surprising. My research on this book led me to his story. I hadn't heard about him either. Not in the media. Not on the news. Not on social media and not from friends. And it's a shame that Titouan Bernicot is not famous because, as far as I'm concerned, he should be. Our media mostly covers the bad news, the horrible, the downtrodden, the sensational, the fringe, and the shameful. It collects views and turns them into impressions to sell advertising.

These media impressions sell valuable ad space, so they stick with it. But what about us? We are left with impressions too – but not the same impressions that marketers sell. We are left with impressions that our world has gone off into the abyss, with no hope. No redemption. No recovery. And the worst part of it all? We begin to believe it. And we start believing that there is no place for us in this world to Just Start and solve problems that are pressing both at work and in the world beyond.

But it doesn't have to be that way. The shame of it all is that the media would just as soon report about rising ocean temperatures and dying coral reefs because sensationalism and disaster stories get those sacred impressions, which are turned into revenue dollars. I argue that if we all Just Start like Titouan Bernicot and many, many others, then we can forever turn the tide and counter all the negativity and filth peddling by making the decision to Just Start on our ideas.

One person can change everything, and that one person could be you.

It is important to note that the Just Start tool is an evolution, not a revolution. This is about small steps that add up incrementally over time. Little by little, they enable you to reach your goal. It is not about an instant result or the instant gratification of meeting your goals. What you are really doing by using the Just Start superpower is enabling momentum in the right direction. We have to have action to begin to use our superpowers, and this is the spark that starts the fire.

No matter how great your dreams, no matter how big your potential, they won't become reality unless you Just Start.

The Just Start superpower is a small step we decide to take that ends up leading to another small step, then another. These steps eventually add up to something significant. Think of the Just Start superpower as a declaration of intent, just like Titouan made on that fateful day when, as a teenager, he decided to fix what was broken. His first step set in motion a lifelong pursuit of meaning, and your first step will do the same for you. But nothing happens until we put it in motion, and we Just Start to realize our potential. You don't have to be some extraordinary genius, prodigy of the business world, or someone rich and famous; you just need to start.

Like you and me, Titouan Bernicot is just a regular person. He is not someone who started with a ton of resources or as the son of an Arab sultan, he is just a regular human being with some gumption to hit the "go" button. His genius is that he gave himself permission to Just Start, and he figured that, along the way, he would learn what he needed when he needed it.

People Just Start all the time in real life and not just to save coral reefs. For instance, those of us who have children or pets or look after an elderly relative know all about it. There is no owner's manual or best practices for having children. You just sort of prepare as best you can and learn as much as you can along the way. You try to raise your children to leave behind a world a bit better than the one you grew up in. I think this is a routine aspiration for parents all over the world, spanning families across the globe. My point is that we need to Just Start sometimes in life without having all the preparation that we think that we need. If we wait until we have enough money, resources, education, connections, or whatever we are waiting for, it may be too late.

Roadblocks

We are resistant to Just Start things in our lives, especially when it comes to business, enterprise, and our careers. We activate a lot of fear – and that fear ends up suffocating us. We fear roadblocks – some of which are imagined, others real. We are so hesitant to open a small business or take that risk on the presentation at work. When it comes to Just Starting, we need to get better at it, and we need to practice it more. We need to learn to see ourselves with the Just Start superpower. Seeing ourselves as creative and innovative human beings is critical to trusting our instinct, which is screaming at us to Just Start.

There are often some real or imagined roadblocks that try to stop us in our tracks. Roadblocks can come in a variety of sizes, but most of them can be categorized as either internal or external roadblocks. Internal roadblocks are ones that we put there ourselves, and external roadblocks are there as a matter of circumstance or byproducts of our pursuit. But all these roadblocks can be overcome by learning to think of ourselves as creative problem solvers and giving ourselves the permission to know that, whatever the roadblock is, we are able to overcome it.

External Roadblocks

External roadblocks often get in the way – throwing us off our course with limitations of some sort – be it resources, access to an advisor or mentor, knowledge of the competition, or much more. In Titouan's case, it was a lack of having the "correct" education in marine biology. Or being told that you are too young. Or being told that there is no way you can do it – you are only one person after all! But really good things begin to happen for us when we Just Start to question someone else's interpretation of what is the "correct" or "best" way to do something.

In Titouan's case, he is making a major impact on the preservation and regrowth of coral reefs in a way other than what is the established norm. And that is exactly what we need to be doing when using our Just Start superpower. When we question what we are told to do – or told not to do – that is when the Just Start superpower is at its best. It enables us to charge forward in the face of what may seem contrary to tradition or the established pathway.

External roadblocks can be tricky. And they can become personal. Some people will spend a lifetime deflecting you from your aspirations simply to fill the vacuum of their own lack of aspiration.

The Just Start superpower will help you overcome all the doubters who may stand in your way. There are tons of people out there who are, for one reason or another, simply miserable. And seeing you succeed with the Just Start superpower will make their blood boil. If we spend our lives listening to others, we never get to experience our true selves and see the power of our own ideas. And that is why I designed the Just Start superpower. I believe that just beneath the surface, every human being has dormant creativity and innovation waiting to burst forth as a force for good – and my mission is to unleash it. I cannot go another day without helping you see how naturally creative you are, how fully capable you are of solving any problem on your own, and how to express that superpower every single day, even when your greatest enemy is yourself.

Internal Roadblocks

Internal roadblocks can be a beast to overcome, but they are also solvable with the Just Start superpower. In the case of internal roadblocks, we are forced to deal with obstacles that we put in our own way. Indeed, we can often be our own worst enemy. And I would argue that internal roadblocks are much more difficult to overcome because they can be cynical and ensconced beliefs that we carry for years deep inside of us. It is the false narrative of what we tell ourselves about ourselves that may be the biggest impediment to using the Just Start superpower. And like arteries in the heart hardened after years of plaque buildup, they are difficult to reverse and clear out.

There are a variety of reasons we put roadblocks in our own way. It can be because we feel we are not worthy of the initiative; it can be because we think that we may fail or not succeed to an acceptable extent; it may be because we overthink the problem and overwhelm ourselves to the point of inaction. Yet in every case, these internal roadblocks can be overcome by learning how to deal with them and pushing ourselves to move forward, even if we are plagued with what we view as internal limitations. How do we do that? By taking the first step.

Taking the First Step

At the end of the day, the Just Start superpower will help overcome even the most ardent naysayers and the most deeply held set of internal obstructions, simply because it moves one thing forward. Just one thing. And knowing that you have taken a step – however small – to move forward is just enough to begin to break through the limitations and restraints that arise both from internal and external roadblocks.

Now I can imagine the cynics and pessimists saying that road-blocks are there for a reason or that an established pathway is the only correct direction we need to take. They might say we need years and years of education to help marine life or that road-blocks are a natural hurdle to progress because they stem from very real limitations. But that would deny the amazing human attribute that we all have deep within to overcome problems of all shapes and sizes. We as humans wouldn't be here on earth if we weren't the most creative and innovative animal species. Throughout human history, there were (and still are) animals that are far faster or far stronger than humans.

But our ability to problem solve a variety of issues and to generate solutions to seemingly impossible problems is exactly what it means to be human. And anyone or anything that seeks to extinguish this light of human ingenuity is going against the grain of what humanity is supposed to do.

This is our role. This is what we are supposed to be doing.

We exist to overcome challenges, to thrive in the face of adversity. And not doing so goes against everything we stand for as human beings. The airplane would never have been invented if the Wright brothers just believed the naysayers or got caught on their own internal or external limitations. The internet wouldn't exist. The computers and satellites reaching the far corners of our solar system and so much more are a result of human ingenuity overcoming obstacles of all kinds to solve problems. And if we just accept that things are hard or difficult and therefore, we don't consider solutions, we go against the very grain of humanity.

Here are a few tools that you can use today to help you Just Start – whether it's that next initiative at work or it's a big challenge going on globally. We need to strengthen our creativity muscles, learning first how to come up with great ideas and then how to get comfortable executing quickly. Quite often, the best way to unlock creativity and deal with all the roadblocks preventing your success is by taking a deep breath and diving right in. So let's go! Let's Just Start with tool #1: Your Week of Ideas.

Tool #1: Your Week of Ideas

The first action-oriented tool we will look at is all about idea generation. This is about learning and appreciating that we are all creative – and indeed you are creative, too. But how do we start? What is that catalyst we need to inspire creativity in us when we may feel that we are indeed not creative?

It turns out that creativity lies in our thoughts. The results of a 2020 study in *Nature Communications*[3] shows us that human beings have an average of 6,000 thoughts per day. That is a lot of thinking. Some of those thoughts are basic and rudimentary, like "I must eat now or scratch that itch on my arm," but others are higher-order thoughts, creative thoughts that we should keep track of. Higher-order thoughts like "I know what presentation we should offer that client," or "I have an idea to help kids process math easier." The mind is always generating thoughts, and it is our duty to pick out the creative ones from the non-creative ones that will help us solve problems both at work and in the world beyond.

Putting Pen to Paper

So how do we separate the creative thoughts from the non-creative thoughts? It's simple. We write things down. Writing things down can be described as nothing less than magical,[4] as the impact on our psychology and physiology is incredible. And two very important things happen when we write things down.

The first thing that happens, according to scientist Mark Murphy,[5] is something called the "External Storage." What that basically means is that writing things down causes you to "store" what you have written down on a piece of paper. It's easy to access – just look at your sheet of paper or notepad.

The second thing that happens is called "encoding." This is when the brain analyzes the input from writing things down in the hippocampus. That part of the brain is responsible for storing long-term memories and making them resistant to forgetting. So when we write things down, we trigger the brain to "encode" into our hippocampus something significant that gives us a higher chance of recall. This is far different from the 6,000 thoughts we have per day. This is telling our brain, "Wait, this idea we wrote down is important. Pay attention."

Yet how many of us write things down? Or much less, do it on a regular basis? With ubiquitous technology everywhere and a cell phone acting as literal extensions of our bodies, our appetite for writing things down on a pad of paper with a pen has dipped to precariously low levels. This poses great peril to our cognitive health. Problems arise when we rely on our technology too much. It's easy, so we do it, but in this case the cost is our creativity and our ability to solve problems.

Scientists call this "Intention Offloading,"[6] and what that basically means is that we offload our memory capabilities, cognition, and our soft skills as human beings away to cold, hard, calculated computer devices we carry around all day, with the pretense that these devices are making our lives better somehow. But they are not.

For example, instead of memorizing where we parked, we use our smartphone tracking feature to remember for us. Or we use the map app in our phone to navigate for us instead of learning the route. Not surprisingly, there are plenty of stories of map apps leading people to drive off a cliff.[7] The problem deepens as we deteriorate our memory and cognition skills by not actively practicing them and using them on a regular basis – choosing instead to offload them to a device, which we think is making our life better. Easier maybe. But better? Certainly not. What we are missing by using technology to offload our abilities is the capability to solve problems with a pen and paper in a way that energizes and cultivates creative thoughts.

Writing Your Lists

With that foundation in place, you're ready to use Your Week of Ideas as a tool for capturing thoughts that prove your creativity, help you Just Start, and provide solutions for challenges at work and beyond.

Start by designating a full seven days. No need for it to be a calendar week; just make sure you know the start and end dates. If it helps you to use Sunday as the start and end date, then certainly do that, but this will work with any of the seven days. Then, commit to carrying a notepad or journal with you wherever you go. It can be a full-sized notepad or something small. If you already carry around your phone with you everywhere you go, this should be an easy addition. Make sure there is a pen you can attach somewhere to that notepad – there are plenty of options available online with pens attached. Finally, every time you get an idea, write it down. It's really that easy. And most importantly, do not edit your thoughts! Just write down different ideas, phrases, concepts, words, sentences, and whatnot as they pop into your mind.

A word of caution. What you will begin to notice as you progress through the seven days of writing is that some of your 6,000 thoughts will seem trivial. You will find yourself writing things like, "Late pick up is on Tuesday" or "Pay the gas bill." But this is normal and in fact a good thing because when we are not editing our thoughts as we write them, sometimes more banal thoughts will get written down. Do not stop the exercise in the middle of the week because you feel as if you are not producing good, worthwhile, or provocative ideas. That will defeat the purpose. Part of the goal of this exercise is to wake ideas that have been dormant for a while, and we cannot do so under pressure. We need to be able to generate ideas freely, without the pressure of conjuring greatness with every thought. It needs to be what it is.

Analyzing Your Lists

At the end of the seven-day period, look at the lists you have made. The first thing to do is to look for any repetitions and patterns. The second thing to do is take note of anything extraordinary, unusual, or out of the ordinary. And finally, the third thing to do is Just Start.

First, have you noticed any patterns with what you have written down with recurring thoughts or ideas? Look past the more plain and everyday thoughts you have written down. Is there anything in there that is an item you keep writing and scribbling about? Is it perhaps time-management related? Like you find that a bunch of your thoughts are related to being late, early, making sure you have enough time, or have spent enough time on particular things? This may indicate to you that the first thing you can Just Start on may be how you view time and how you manage it to get more done. Or are you seeing perhaps items that repeat related to a particular client or process you keep thinking about? Like you have noticed that you keep writing down "automation" or "maximizing efficiencies" or something like that? Perhaps it is time to Just Start on an idea to streamline some process or look at approaching a pathway differently.

Now, let's look for anything out of the ordinary. Continuing from the examples above, let's say most of your thoughts are around time management, lack of time, too much time, being late, and so on. But you notice that on Wednesday of that Week of Ideas you wrote down something unusual – like "forget about the money invested and just make it the best it can be." Perhaps this is an idea you need to Just Start. Worrying less about costs and more about quality. These ideas will eventually tie into something that is going on in your work life and beyond. It's up to you to find it.

Writing things down helps unleash a torrent of creative thoughts; sometimes the best are found outside the patterns and norms that we have written down. Or if you keep writing down "automation" or "efficiency" like the example above, and you notice that a few times you wrote "freeform" or "let it go," perhaps this is a good time to Just Start an idea about empowering people or letting go of rigid guidelines.

Finally, let's Just Start. Pick and choose one idea and propose starting it in some way, shape, or form. Remember, these ideas all start small at first and build over time. Titouan did not launch his company overnight – it took many years and many small steps to get there. Use your Week of Ideas as small stepping stones and little increments to make significant progress on your creativity.

Tool #2: Imagine the Worst

When I ask my keynote audience to think of the worst possible thing that could happen if they execute a particular idea, any idea, I often hear things like, "I'm gonna get fired," or "My boss is gonna kill me." Sometimes these fears are about something that might really happen; often times they are not. We regularly have a great idea, only to immediately think, "I'm never gonna get to do this. There's not enough time, money, or organizational support." But it turns out that none of those things are actual roadblocks.

Success and Failure

Fear can be a crippling debilitator at work, taking one of two main forms. One is the fear of success, the other is the fear of failure.

The fear of success often blocks us from becoming who we really are, simply because we are too afraid to become it. Sometimes the fear comes from being too afraid to try an initiative because we fear that we would be successful, and that success would somehow take us out of our comfort zone.[8] We are paralyzed with fear that may lead us to successful places in our lives because we don't know what to do if that success actually materializes.

Fear of failure is a fear of what will happen if we attempt a particular goal or initiative and then fail to achieve the desired outcome. A recent study found that more than 40% of people at work have a fear of failure.[9] And the numbers increase even more when looking at highly educated professionals in the workforce.

No matter what the fear is, whether it is a fear of failure or a fear of success, we can overcome those fears by using my second action tool, which is Imagine the Worst. This is all about is trying to Imagine the Worst possible outcome of Just Starting on a particular path. And this is important because it may just clear out a roadblock that is stopping you from starting. We need to identify the potential risks before launching forward as we face them head on. And in that, we will realize they are not as scary as we think.

Flipping the Script

What I'd like you to do is think about something from your list of ideas that sounds good to you – an idea that you would like to start. Now we will play a bit of a detective game in which we try to identify all potential threats to this idea – all potential risks that may occur if we launch forward. In the same way that you wrote down Your Week of Ideas, write down all the fears, risks, and threats that you can come up with if you were to try that particular idea.

Now imagine the absolute worst. What can happen if you take part in this idea of yours? Is it getting fired? Is it potentially losing your credibility or standing in the organization? I doubt it. More than likely, your fear is really not all that rational. It's probably an overreaction laced with fear that stops you from moving forward.

Now how do I know that? Because we humans often let even the smallest chance of danger fill us with fear, we end up feeling overwhelmed. And that overwhelming feeling drives fear into our hearts. And in an endless cycle that feeds itself, we dive deeper and deeper into despair, not realizing that the fear we have built up is most likely irrational and non-existent. In Dan Arieley's book *Predictably Irrational*, he determines, through numerous scientific experiments and findings, that irrationality governs much of human behavior in systematic and predictable ways. And he has built a career on challenging the assumption that humans make decisions based on rational thought.

What we should do instead is rearrange our thoughts to understand that perhaps Imagining the Worst is just that: an imagination of the worst. And that imagination is not real. The extremes our mind takes us to is highly unlikely to occur, if ever. We need to instead rearrange our thoughts to find the good and decency in our ideas and understand that the irrational reaction is often incorrect. More than likely our fear is governing some great ideas, and it shouldn't be that way. That fear leads us to cheat ourselves out of a meaningful and robust existence simply because we are fearing the worst. We can instead choose to rearrange our thoughts to allow our ideas to have a chance to materialize.

We need to flip the script on fear and instead look at what may happen if we don't take a risk on our ideas. What will we be missing out on if we don't Take a Chance? What great thing will we never get to experience because of that fear? Are you willing to risk it? I sure am not. And I hope you are not either.

Taking a Chance on our idea is essential in making the world go round. When we face our fear head on, and Imagine the Worst, we can then see that our brain goes to that giant stack of bad thoughts and only sees a very, very small sliver of hope for the good. Using the Imagine the Worst tool will help us see our world more clearly, revealing that our worst fear is highly unlikely. Learning how to rearrange our thoughts, so the bad stack gets smaller and the good stack gets larger, is essential.

Your idea deserves to be out in the world. Don't limit it because of fear.

Tool #3: Own the Transition

There is a very interesting period between the generation of an idea and the execution of that idea that I call the transition. Quite literally, the transition is a period of action that moves an idea into reality. It is the last step in the Just Start superpower, allowing us to transition from an idea in our head to an idea out in the world.

Most people find themselves at two extremes during the transition: they either have so many ideas that they don't know where to start or what idea to transition into reality, or they have such precious few ideas that they are not willing to transition into the world and ultimately hesitate to Just Start. But Owning the Transition can be an incredibly powerful action tool that comes from the Just Start superpower, and this is where the rubber really meets the road.

We have, at this point, made a list of our Week of Ideas, and identified some tantalizing prospects. Then, we banished fear by Imagining the Worst and finding out that it is unlikely to happen because it is more likely a product of irrational thinking and fear. Finally, we need to Own the Transition – that sacred space between an idea and execution – so that we can Just Start to see our ideas out there in the world.

Stepping Outside Your Comfort Zone

We own our transition by picturing our Just Start moment as stepping outside of our comfort zone and into this new zone of transition, even if that step out of our comfort zone is a small one. A recent amazing study found that participants had greater learning potential by simply stepping outside their comfort zone.[10] So stepping outside our comfort zone allows us to transition into trying out our Just Start idea in the real world.

So how do we do it? We identify the transition point that is giving us so much grief and turn that grief point into an action item. It's the exact point that makes you uncomfortable about trying out an idea, no matter what it is. For example, let's say that you have an idea but you are reluctant to transition that idea because it requires you to take a flight, make a phone call, or for some other reason. Maybe you hate planes because they are dirty and loud. Or maybe you hate calling people because it's awkward to you and you prefer to text. These examples are concrete transition points that are giving you anguish. Just thinking about what makes you uncomfortable is not enough; it will cause you to spin out of control, forever paralyzed by your own indecision in an endless cycle of inaction. So this step has to uncover an action that you can take to overcome that discomfort. Just one action.

At first, taking that flight or making that first phone call seems uncomfortable, and we don't like that. But turning that discomfort into an action item is critical. This is where we need to "transition" by taking that flight or making that phone call. When we recognize that our fear of taking the flight or making the phone call is simply discomfort—and that the discomfort is fleeting—we can face it more easily. The more we practice, the more comfortable we become, until eventually we Own the Transition. Finally, we realize the things that we made mountains of are molehills.

We like comfortable and predictable, but nothing ever will happen for you and your ideas if you stay in your comfort zone. So identifying what specific item is bothering you and stopping you from transitioning that idea into reality is key. And assigning some action item to overcome it is critical. Then doing it until it is no longer uncomfortable is how you get that idea out into the real world.

I am willing to bet that if you break down your initiative and identify the exact point at which you will get uncomfortable, then overcoming that discomfort is not too big a deal. If you absolutely hate cold calling, but your idea is to get more business through outreach to untapped leads, then break down that cold call into a "transition" step that will start you doing that particular task. What about cold calling is so hard for you? The answer will be different for everyone.

But now, instead of getting lost in your head forever thinking about your overwhelmed feeling, assign an action item to deal with that cold call. Perhaps it's to make one cold call. Perhaps it's to call a known contact and alternate between cold calls and warm leads. Each specific "transition" will vary. Once you deal with your uncomfortable transition with some action item that makes sense, doing it a second time becomes easier. The third time even easier. Eventually, in no time, you will no longer be uncomfortable with solely cold calling potential prospects.

Break the situation down into a single, manageable step. Instead of feeling overwhelmed, focus on the one thing that's keeping you from moving forward. Maybe it's sending that "transition" email or starting that transition 45-minute walk in the morning to begin an exercise regimen. No matter what that transition is, it is born out of our dislike of being uncomfortable, but the amazing thing about human beings is our infinite ability to be adaptable. And in that adaptability, we can uncover a new reality where what we once thought would make us uncomfortable is now something that we can derive joy from.

Finding the Path Forward

I have a consulting client who had wanted for years to ask a vendor to make her a product. She had a really good idea to partner with the vendor to fill a shortage in her particular industry and thought that this vendor would be a great partner in producing the part. She did everything right to Just Start: she made a list of ideas and came up with the idea for the equipment, imagined the worst and overcame it, only to get stuck in the transition.

I asked her what was the one thing that made her particularly uncomfortable to transition her idea into reality? Well in this case it was something some people would view as minor – but nonetheless it mattered to her and was her own personal transition issue. She would have to physically meet a vendor she never met before in person, which could be awkward, strange, and take her out of her comfort zone.

So, we broke the transition down into one step that she could overcome, albeit uncomfortably, to transition the idea into motion. The action item was that she decided she would be able to go to a lunch meeting if it were at a familiar location – taking some of the sting out. So she did just that, and we were able to transition the idea into reality.

The vendor ended up loving the idea and producing the part, and she managed to establish a partnership with that vendor where they profit share that new equipment in any market it sells into. And all this could have not happened simply because there was anxiety around the transition.

However big or small the transition issue is, it needs to be overcome in some way that makes sense to you. And no matter what is stopping you from not wanting to make that phone call to not wanting to travel or even not wanting to meet in person, it will be different for everyone. And that's okay. Because the goal is to transition an idea into reality, not to judge ourselves for not getting the transition done in the first place. There is no one-size-fits-all with a transition, and what may seem insurmountable to you may be a cakewalk for someone else. None of that matters as the expression of creativity is personal to us all, and ultimately finding the path forward to overcome your transition is your personal journey. Find whatever may be blocking your transition, add an action item, and off you go bringing ideas out into the real world.

Conclusion

In this chapter we looked at the first superpower and all the ways to Just Start an idea and make it a reality. We looked at ways to come up with ideas, ways to Imagine the Worst so that we can let our ideas roam free from irrationality, and how to take those ideas and make the rubber meet the road as we transition our ideas into the real world. Next, we'll explore another crucial superpower – one that extends the Just Start mindset into understanding that the most important investment you'll ever make, at work and beyond, is simple: the investment you make in yourself.

2

Superpower #2: Invest in Yourself

What Renewable Forests and Bourbon Teach Us About the Long Term in a Short-Term World

We make fine bourbon at a profit if we can, at a loss if we must, but always fine bourbon.

—Pappy Van Winkle

Julian Van Winkle III is the first James Beard award winner from Kentucky.[1] The James Beard Award is given to outstanding contributions in the culinary arts. But Julian is not a chef. He has no restaurant. He is not a baker. What Julian does is make bourbon, and not just any bourbon.

Julian is the third-generation Van Winkle to produce bourbon whiskey in Kentucky. In order for whiskey to be called bourbon, it has to adhere to some pretty strict protocols. It has to be made with at least 51% corn, aged in charred new oak barrels, made in the United States (most bourbon comes from Bourbon Country in Kentucky), distilled to a maximum of 160 proof, and bottled between 80 and 150 proof.

While that may sound like a lot of requirements, Julian takes them to the next level. He is known for exceeding the requirements in making one of the finest bourbons anywhere in the world at the famous Old Rip Van Winkle Distillery. Some of the bourbon he makes spends over 20 years maturing before it's ready to be sold to customers. This is one of the rarest and most sought-after bourbons in the world, and people often pay well into the five figures for just one bottle, if you can even manage to find a bottle to purchase. He makes bourbon in the family tradition that stretches back over 100 years, taking great pains to make the spirit as good as it can possibly be with a combination of artistry, science, deep aging, and regular tastings. And if that is not enough in making excellent bourbon, he (and other excellent distillers) hope that their bourbon "makes the trip" given all the things they have to endure to make their stellar product.

What "making the trip" is all about is the hope that the bourbon matures properly. Bourbon takes many years to develop into something spectacular, and Julian hopes that he can stack the deck in his favor so that he has the best chances of his bourbon making the long trip through the years into something worthy of the family name. The long road is fraught with peril. The variables that can go wrong as bourbon "makes the trip" are staggering in both complexity and scope. Barrels can be too hot or too cold, improperly stored or rotated. Leaks may let water in or bourbon out, or, heaven forbid, a fire could break out in the warehouse. There are countless other factors that can prevent an Old Rip Van Winkle from completing its journey worthy of praise. In that way, making bourbon is a lot like life. It has some science to it and some art, and a bit of luck too. And we never really quite know how things will turn out.

Given that the average life cycle of what Julian makes is often between 12 and 23 years, what Julian bottles today just may well outlive him. Yet he does it every day without hesitation. Having the foresight to Invest in Yourself (our second superpower) in making a product and process that he may never realize himself but a future generation would is exactly the point, ensuring quality and building something that matters in the long run. It's all about the long game. It's all about Investing in Yourself.

Julian's grandfather, Pappy, who started the distillery in 1893[2] was famous for saying, "We make fine bourbon at a profit if we can, at a loss if we must, but always fine bourbon." The entire existence of the company was to continually invest in the most important thing that you can ever possibly invest in. And that is our second superpower: Investing in Yourself.

At each step of the way Julian, his father, or his grandfather could take the shortcut or the easy way out. Perhaps compromise on an ingredient or pull that barrel just a bit early for maximum profitability over quality. Or they could have lowered their standards by not tasting as often or releasing in a shorter span of time, but at each step, the overiding desire to invest in themselves and ignore outside forces has consistently beat out all the other options and remained steadfast in an ever-changing world. Like the bourbon, this tradition has "made the trip" into every corner of the company and now lives on with Julian's son, Preston, the fourth in the line of crafting superb bourbon. He is always guided by the key principle of continually Investing in Yourself and playing the long game – regardless of the fashions of the day or fleeting trends.

Today the selection of premium Van Winkle bourbons are among some of the most highly desired spirits in the world. And that attention to quality at each step by continually Investing in Yourself has paved a path of sustainability that is the envy of the industry.

The Paper Industry's Long Game

What does the paper industry have to do with Julian Van Winkle's small bourbon company? Well, it turns out quite a bit. Both industries are continually dedicated to investing in themselves to sustain long-term success. Yet at first glance it may not appear that way.

When thinking of the paper industry, the first feeling that hits most of us is guilt.[3,4] Recent studies have shown that we associate feelings of guilt with the perceived impression of depleting natural resources. And the paper industry feels like an industry bent on depleting natural resources. We feel that ping of guilt as we remember our second-grade science class where we learned that paper comes from trees, that wood from a tree is chipped and ground down into pulp and dried into sheets. We feel guilty because images of heavy machinery clear-cutting forests come to mind, polluting the ground and leaving an otherwise pristine forest in waste, a ghost of its former self. At least that's what I thought before I began this research for my keynotes and this book. Yet it turns out this vision is completely false. There is hope out there – and it is impressive.

Hope comes in the form of the industry's "managed forests." A "managed forest" is a forest area, much like what you envision in the mind's eye when thinking about a forest, where companies intentionally plant, care for, and harvest trees with the goal of producing goods that consume the entire life cycle of wood products. From the branches to the leaves, to the stump and trunk. It really is an incredible concept. Companies literally plant trees and harvest them to use for particular needs, and much like bourbon, some of these trees take a generation or more to mature, making the imperative of the industry to continually invest in themselves.

In the case of the paper industry, which follows certain certifications,[5] a successful implementation of Investing in Yourself gives the industry true and real sustainability while still managing to give us the products that we all use every day. It's a win-win. We all benefit from having more trees around as they help sop up carbon dioxide and a variety of other airborne toxins. Plus, the trees in the managed forests provide a habitat for wildlife.

Yet the news gets even better. Wood now makes its way into a ton of everyday products outside the paper industry. Trees are processed into lumber, housing materials, and a myriad of other uses like aspirin, wine corks, and latex, and others less commonly known like Rayon, sponges, and tires. The Michelin tire company[6] is studying the impact of using wood pulp to replace oil-based derivatives in a new elastomer compound used to make tires. This creative approach one day may change the future of the tire industry forever – away from oil to trees that come from managed forests.

We rely heavily on trees for so many needs, both inside and outside of the paper industry. Yet every step of the way, managed forests are leading to a sustainable environment, where the very act of Investing in Yourself as an industry has led to the planting of more and more trees, which everyone can agree is a good thing.

Here are some impressive facts:

- Each year, the United States plants over 1 billion trees.[7] For over 50 consecutive years, the country has had a net forest growth that superseded annual forest harvests due to sustainable "managed forests."

- In North America (that means Canada and Mexico too), many more trees are grown than are harvested (think about that for a second). Our forests have become renewable resources simply because we have chosen to invest in ourselves and use a "managed forest" approach to help us get there.

- The net growth of U.S. forests has been – get ready for it – steadily growing for at least a hundred years and is now on track to *grow* roughly 2% every 10 years through the practice of Investing in Yourself by planting acre after acre of "managed forests."

- Trees are one of the best tools humanity has for overcoming global climate change, and contrary to what you may hear in the media, the paper industry is creating quite an impact while still managing to supply products, make a profit, and clean up the air.

The concept of managed forests and playing the long game is always top of mind in the paper and bourbon industries for different reasons. In bourbon, it's about quality that takes time. And in the paper industry, it's making sure tomorrow's paper needs are met by what we plan for today. Now, all of this Investing in Yourself has gotten me thinking a lot about the language of permission and the Ten Commandments.

The Language of Permission

To be able to tap into your most creative self, you must Invest in Yourself. This means doing the work now that will help you think creatively in the long run. This means putting resources into yourself now, today, that you may not see a return on for 5, 10, even 30 years. This means giving yourself the permission and space to plant the ideas now and watch them grow tomorrow.

Creative problem solving requires the type of thinking that Julian uses daily at his distillery and that companies like International Paper use in their managed forests. It is about doing the work now to enable rewards later. And the way you Invest in Yourself may look different from how Julian or International Paper practices it – and that's okay. It's part of the shift in mindset from immediate gratification to long, sustained success. It is a concept even found in one of humankind's most sacred texts, the Bible.

The Hebrew Bible[8] teaches in Proverbs 22:8 that, "He who sows injustice will reap violence" in that any plans laid in ill will eventually manifest further into viciousness. I like this quote because it clearly shows what we shouldn't do – violence – while giving readers permission to interpret for themselves what we should do instead. It specifically outlines what is forbidden, but it leaves open what is not forbidden. I call this the *language of permission*.

The language of permission is a subset of the Invest in Yourself superpower because it allows every idea you can possibly think of to be used to solve any problem. This is a very interesting differentiator in developing and maintaining a Solution Mindset. And it works like this:

What is not expressly off-limits is allowable. Think of that for a second. Whatever is not expressly a limitation is now an opportunity for you to solve a problem.

For example, let's say you are a farmer in a particular area, and the laws of the county say that you cannot plant a certain seed. Let's call that disallowed seed Seed A. That pretty much means you can't plant Seed A in your area. Some people stop right there and throw up their hands and exclaim, "We can't plant Seed A. We're stuck. That's the rule, and we have to stick to it." But when we look at this with a Solution Mindset, we choose to see this rule as full of permission. How? By choosing to plant perhaps Seed B or Seeds C, D, E, and so on. You may even want to plant established small plants, bypassing seeds altogether. The language of permission sees what is possible instead of getting stuck on what is not possible.

The 10 Commandments do the same thing. Most are written with the language of permission, a "don't" instead of a "do." This offers an entirely creative construct that allows us to find opportunities to everyday problems. The language of permission is a way to frame any issue or problem that allows for the most possible creative solutions. So instead of telling us what to do, the 10 Commandments[9] mostly tell us what not to do. And that is a huge difference. Before we get much further, here are the 10 Commandments, because I have found recent research showing that only 6% of people can name all 10.[10] Here they are, based on Chabad.org's translation, in case you have forgotten:

(1) Thou shalt have no other Gods before Me.

(2) Thou shalt not make any idols or graven images.

(3) Thou shalt not take the name of the Lord thy God in vain.

(4) Remember the Sabbath day to keep it holy.

(5) Honor thy father and thy mother.

(6) Thou shalt not murder.

(7) Thou shalt not commit adultery.

(8) Thou shalt not steal.

(9) Thou shalt not bear false witness against thy neighbor.

(10) Thou shalt not covet anything that belongs to thy neighbor.

Look at them closely. Eight out of 10 of them, a whopping 80%, expressly put things off-limits. But what is not off-limits, is not a violation of the Commandments. In other words, there is very little here (only two Commandments) on what we should do, and a bunch more Commandments (eight of them) on what we shouldn't do. Boiled down to its essence, if it's not expressly off-limits, and it makes sense, then go for it. The language of permission written into the 10 Commandments is the ability to do just about anything that is not expressly off-limits. What would happen if you were to apply this at your work or in your career or business? For that matter, even the two commandments above that tell you to do things don't tell you *how* to do them. You can honor your father and mother however you want. The language of permission is implicitly possible both when you are told what you cannot do and when you are told what you can.

If we choose to reap our rewards, no matter what we seek, we need to sow now to benefit later. If it's not disallowed expressly, then it's allowed. If it's required, then adjust *how exactly* you carry it out. In the very literal sense, the paper companies we featured earlier plant trees today so that in 20 years they can reap the benefits. There is no precedence for that – no rule that says you can't plant trees today for the future. They made it up because it was good for business. And, in turn, it is good for the world. This is what they have come up with to save their own livelihood, and it's pretty terrific for the earth, too.

Same with Julian and Pappy Van Winkle. He makes bourbon now that will hopefully "make the trip" to benefit the future an entire generation from now. Long after he has passed. He does it for quality reasons and tradition, but there is no rule that says you must mature bourbon for 23 years to reap its benefit. In fact, when he took over from his father, the longest time Pappy was maturing the bourbon was 10 years. He introduced the 23-year-aged bourbon because there was no rule that said he couldn't do it, so he did it. That's the language of permission.

But far too often people are hesitant to use the language of permission and invest in themselves to create a Solution Mindset at work and beyond. And the reasons can be surprising.

Why Are We So Hesitant to Invest in Ourselves?

Why are we so hesitant to reap what we sow and use the language of permission to invest today in things that tomorrow will give us great benefit? Why not exploit the language of permission to allow us to invest in ourselves and make that investment today for our future?

We are hesitant to invest in ourselves for two primary reasons. The first reason we don't invest in ourselves is that most of us are terrified of breaking the rules. We live in very orderly societies, with clear rules, and we understand them. And breaking them seems so scary that we don't use the language of permission to even poke around a bit and see what is possible within the construct of what is expressly off limits. Second, we are just so bad about investing today for our future. Especially financially. Studies repeatedly show that saving now for later, in any form, is excruciatingly difficult for humans to do. For instance, a recent Pew Charitable Trust study[11] found that 51%[12] of Americans worry that they'll run out of money when they're no longer earning a paycheck at work, and 70%[13] of retirees wish they had started saving earlier. We're pretty bad at investing today for the future, and we need to get better at investing in ourselves to realize our #2 superpower. The good news is that we can learn to overcome these two issues.

To unpack the first reason that most of us are terrified of breaking rules, we must begin to look at rules as an absolute targeted mandate, not a wide-cast net. What I mean by this is we need to begin to look at rules in our careers or businesses as ultra-specific niche details expressly about what we cannot do – a law. Like it says in the 10 Commandments, we cannot steal. Now, let's take stealing: can we loan money at a profit? Sure. Not expressly outlawed so it's okay. We didn't steal money; we are loaning it at an advantage to us. Can we borrow innovation from one industry and apply it in ours? Sure. We can't steal another industry's patented innovation and apply it to ours, but we can borrow that approach and use our own creativity to find within that rule everything that is not expressly disallowed. It turns out that in any rule there is a ton of permission there. We just need to get comfortable learning how to look and asking questions.

In examining the second reason that we're bad about investing for our future, the research shows us that investing in ourselves is just plain hard work, and studies show it may be related to our self-esteem. One recent study[14] showed that a lowering of self esteem is directly correlated with a lower propensity to Invest in Yourself. And it turns out that one of the reasons we have so much trouble investing in ourselves is because we cannot see, touch, or feel this investment; there is no instant gratification. We tend to like things that give us an immediate gain, yet investing in ourselves is not immediate. It takes time.

One of my favorite studies[15] has shown that when offered a choice between two payoffs, one that can occur immediately but is small, and one that is delayed but much larger, people tend to choose the smaller, earlier payout! Crazy right? Nope. It's who we are as humans. Yet simply being aware of the fact that we have the proclivity to take the lower payout because it is instant can sway us to make a better choice to harness the second superpower of investing in ourselves and playing the long game.

The best part is that all the limitations holding you back from Investing in Yourself are surmountable. Tapping into our creative and innovative abilities to invest in ourselves is not only possible but is also likely when using the three concrete tools described in the following sections. So, let's jump in with the first tool, Start on the Five.

Tool #1: Start on the Five

The first tool we will look at is all about time management. Not all investments have to take 20 years. Sometimes, you only need five minutes to encourage creative thinking and problem-solving. But the challenge is that we often don't even take five minutes to pause and invest in ourselves. We need to take the time. That's true even if perhaps you are like me, and your day runs into endless meetings, one after the other. If that weren't enough, often I find myself being double booked and sometimes even triple booked in timeslots of endless meetings. It's a miracle that any work actually gets done having spent so much time in meetings. But there is a way to cope, and it comes in the form of Start on the Five.

Start on the Five is a technique that allows the brain critical rest before diving into task after task. Studies from Microsoft[16] have shown that this critical brain rest is necessary for healthy brain function but also for idea generation. The study says that, based on brainwave activity, Microsoft found that back-to-back meetings are stressful and that short breaks are necessary to improve our ability to focus and engage. And finally, breaks between meetings and tasks in the workplace allow for your brain to reset[17] for a brief moment, allowing the cumulative stress of all those back-to-back meetings to be reduced.

So how do we do this? How do we allow our brains to get that much-needed rest to be able to invest in ourselves to be more energized, creative, and involved at work? We do it by starting our meetings on the five.

What this basically means, for example, is that instead of having meetings from 1 p.m. to 2 p.m., we start the meeting at 1:05 and we end it at 2:00 p.m. Then the next meeting will not start until 2:05 and it will run to 2:30, even if it's supposed to be a half hour (it's really 25 minutes). And so on for the rest of the day. Always Start on the Five. Building in that five minutes of break is critical for the brain to reset and have a chance to consume all the information that was shared in the meeting.

This five-minute break gives people time to process and reflect, "What's the subject of this meeting? What would I like the outcome to be? What is the problem that needs to be solved?" Or this break can allow you to shut down, giving your mind a chance to be still. The small investment of only five minutes allows you to be better equipped to come up with creative solutions. This tool is about taking a five-minute investment in yourself to commit to being more creative and innovative, building your Solution Mindset. This doesn't just apply to meetings. You can use this in any work environment where you feel like your brain is running non-stop on the same hamster wheel. The important thing is to take five minutes for a mental reset.

Most people don't take the time that needs to be invested to come up with ideas that can help solve problems at work and beyond. But if we force ourselves to Start on the Five and take that five minutes away from endless task-based work, we allow some space for creativity and innovation. We make time to think.

It is my hope that this five minutes is the very first increment of time investment you choose to make in yourself to allow your ideas to flourish. Then over time, grow the five minutes into a deeper and more significant investment of time. Learning to take time out for idea generation is truly a measure of Investing in

Yourself and giving yourself the time you need not only to function in a world that moves at breakneck speeds, but also to invest time to cultivate your ideas to see them into reality.

Tool #2: Take That Class Already

When I conduct keynotes for corporate clients and associations, I usually ask the group of attendees about a wish list of classes they want to take. Most times, this question brings up smiles across the room, and I have been in some very tough rooms. Almost universally, everyone wants to take a class of some sort. And people around the room, whether it's a ballroom with thousands or a boardroom with a handful of people, instantly light up when they hear this question.

Now why do people smile when they hear this question? Why are people moved to grin at the mere suggestion of taking some type of class or course they have always wanted to take? Because it's fun. I suspect it's because everyone, no matter who you are, has always wanted to take some sort of class as an adult. Perhaps it is the fond memories of school. Perhaps it's an attempt to advance at work with a new certification. Perhaps it's about embracing the fact that we are all wired for creativity and this question harkens back to primordial humans, intent on maintaining creativity as part of human survival.

No matter when and where this question is asked, hands go up. People from all walks of life, from frontline employees to the C-suite, all have some activity or class that they have always wanted to take. Whether it's a fitness class or a diving certification for their next vacation. Maybe it's a PMP certification to be a Project Management Professional or an auto detailing class where you learn how to polish your car.

But now comes the uncomfortable part. Inevitably, when folks are finished sharing what class they want to take, I ask a follow-up question. And this is where the smiles disappear and the good feelings begin to melt away.

I follow up and ask the one question I already know the answer to – and that question is the theme of this second tool in the Investing in Yourself superpower: I ask folks to raise their hand if they actually did take that wine-making class or art course. And I scan the room.

I am lucky to see two or three hands go up, even in a room of thousands. Such precious few of us make the time to invest in ourselves by taking that class that we have been wanting to take for a number of years, and the results are often detrimental, not only to our mental health, but to our ability to become creative and innovative.

The challenge here is not really about taking a class. Sure, that's part of it, but the challenge here is making time for something that we *want* to do. The effort, in itself, is the reward. We all know the excuses and believe me I get it: we don't have the time. We'll take that class in a month, six months . . . but somehow years go by and we haven't taken a leap on that idea, that thing we wanted to do, that vacation we wanted to go on, or taking time to visit with our friends from high school. And sadly, most of us never end up taking that class because we push it off to tomorrow. And tomorrow never comes.

Allowing yourself the freedom to take that class or to go on that vacation and making time for something that you want to do means that indeed you are Investing in Yourself. And the results of that investment may seem trivial at first. For instance, you may think that taking that cooking class or sip-and-paint class has little to do with anything but a bit of fun. But that simple task of stepping out of your comfort zone and trying something new can have transformative effects. And it creates a repeatable behavior pattern – a habit – where you indeed make the time to Invest in Yourself. And you will continue to do so in other ways as part of a new behavior pattern that is beneficial. Taking these different classes or doing these different activities develops skills, awareness, new perspectives, and so much more that you will actually use, even unconsciously, in the workplace. You don't even have to try to apply that cool little nugget you picked up at the auto detailing class about separating your tools to apply this to your job as a nurse, for example. This will happen automatically, as if by osmosis, simply because you made the effort.

If you have given yourself the permission to take that class in the first place, maybe now you will give yourself the permission to invest in the long term at work. Like a muscle that needs to be used in order to get stronger, the more we make investments in ourselves, the more we get used to the process. Make some time. Take that class now.

Tool #3: Make Time for *Your* Big Idea

We spend a lot of time at work trying to please our boss, our shareholders, our managers – and all the bosses above our boss – in an endless pursuit to measure up to expectations. We try really hard to do a good job, but sometimes in doing that we miss out on individual creativity that we can bring to the tasks we fulfill. We become so focused on giving the higher-ups what they need that our own ideas get put on the back burner. We feel like we're powerless and have no control over work priorities or how our time is spent.[18] But we do have control, and it's time to Make Time for *Your* Big Idea.

Investing in your own ideas at work should be one of your biggest priorities. I understand that you may be in middle management or a frontline employee and feel that you cannot influence big ideas at work. There is a question I get in nearly every keynote I conduct, and the question is always centered around innovating and creating when not in a leadership position: is it possible to think creatively about solutions when I am not in charge? How can I be creative at work when I'm not the boss? Well, here is a tool that you can use, no matter where you are in the structure of the company, to exercise your Solution Mindset.

How can we do this? The concept around this tool is all about finding a way to deliver whatever your task is – and then finding a way to add a version that is satisfactory to you: a new and different version full of your ideas, not your bosses' ideas, not your company's ideas, not your shareholder's ideas. Your ideas.

Here's how it works: You create two different versions of the same task deliverable. For example, let's say that you write a report. You do it the same way each month, the way your boss wants you to. But you hate the report because you have some ideas for how to make it better. So instead of brooding about how much your job sucks and how you get no freedom to improve things at work, just create two versions of that same report: one the way you were asked to do it, and one in the way you want to do it – full of your own ideas.

For example, let's say that you hate the monthly report specifically because it does not paint an accurate picture of the latest research of new client initiatives. So first you write what your boss asked, then you research new initiatives or new client groups in that different way that you want and put it into this second version – a new version – with all of your fresh, new, and different ideas of what a great monthly report should look like.

Can you image how incredible our lives at work and beyond would be if we were to implement this? Even if we were to do this on a few assignments, a quarter of the impact would be enormous. Having led companies and staff for many years, I know that sometimes folks get stuck at work. They feel that their boss is not innovative or receptive to new and different ideas.

So, they figure that they don't have any opportunities to invest in themselves at work and instead burn out, get disconnected and disinterested, and start to pull back on any new and fresh ideas. Perhaps this is what you are doing at work today. When I ask folks why it is that they do this, they say that basically their ideas are not well received at work and they don't want to be in an environment where creativity and innovation are stifled. And therefore, they stop sharing ideas and thoughts around any initiatives that they feel can be improved or enhanced in any way to make things better.

The core problem with this logic is that we cannot wait to find an ideal employment situation – or the perfect hotbed of innovation. It simply does not exist. We need to be creative and innovative no matter what. It's who we are as human beings and is as essential to our well-being as water and food, especially in companies and organizations that are not creative. We need to continually innovate and try our ideas, even when we are not "given permission."

What we instead need to do is make time for our big idea by delivering the request – no matter what it is – and then immediately (or simultaneously) making a second version full of our own unique ideas. That way we are still in compliance with whatever the task is, and have completed that task, but also hold in our back pocket a version that features our ideas, our approach, our thoughts, our pathways. The beauty of this tool is that most of the time, our ideas outshine the initial request. Our version of the research to the new client group is way better than what was asked of us because it includes our own creative view of what we plan to achieve. And we get excited about doing the work because it is our work. We take ownership of it because it features our beliefs and our ideas.

Another side benefit of doing this is that our version of the task is free from pressure, stress, and the burden to get it right. When we have a task already done that we have executed, we can always use that as the "back up" to our ideas or our version – and we don't feel much pressure and worry about getting our version totally right or making it perfect, because our version is the cherry on top – the version that we can have *fun* putting together. There is always the safe way out – what the boss asked us to do – and our version is just an extra effort of creativity and innovation that lies within us taking time to invest in ourselves and our ideas.

Now you can decide if you want to show your version of the report or whatever it is to your boss/coworkers/clients – or not. You can take parts of the new version or use the whole thing. Sometimes our new creative versions will be well received, occasionally not. But that is not the point. When we use tool #3, we find that we are much happier at work.

Occasionally, folks tell me that doing two versions of one assignment sounds like double the workload. And in an already taxed work environment, finding the time to do so is difficult. But I would argue that not finding the time to execute a task in your own personal creative innovative way takes more work, because you cheat yourself out of the very best use of superpower #2, which is to Invest in Yourself and in your own ideas! Sure, it may seem like extra work, but that extra work literally is an investment in ourselves.

If you continually look to others to "allow" you to be creative or innovative, or wait for the perfect time to try something new or share that idea, it will never come. The ideal situation simply does not exist, so making the most of your own abilities and investing the time and effort it takes in your own versions of assignments is perhaps one of the most powerful implementations of Investing in Yourself that you can possibly undertake at work.

The point of this tool is not to inject ideas into a stagnant workplace but to exercise our own ideas so that our creativity muscle gets used repeatedly, and we build new behavior patterns that allow us to keep an agile mind, exercised and practiced. And that gives us great personal joy and satisfaction and the self-confidence to realize that our ideas are worthwhile and important. No matter what anyone says.

Conclusion

In this chapter we looked at the second superpower and all the ways to Invest in Yourself for the long-term. We looked at ways to make little investments in time, ways to take classes we have been wanting to take for a long time, and finally how to make room for our own ideas, no matter what, at work and beyond. Now we are going to look at another very important superpower that will drive the Invest in Yourself capabilities into new realms. We will look at how Using a Filter, the third superpower, may just help filter out distractions, enabling a Solution Mindset full of robust, novel, and life-changing ideas.

CHAPTER

3

Superpower #3: Use a Filter

What Life-Saving Innovations for Cleaning Dirty Water Teach Us About Unblocking Our Creative Thinking

Light itself is a great corrective. A thousand wrongs and abuses that are grown in darkness disappear like owls and bats before the light of day.

—President James A. Garfield

Dr. Moshe Frommer should have been a rabbi. He spent his youth in schools studying the Torah with other eager students, looking to extract new meaning from every word.[1] That was the path his uncle took, and that was the path he was expected to take. In the world of biblical studies, discoveries are not the latest new products or services. The discoveries there come from the extraction of as much meaning as possible from words written in antiquity. The goal is to examine each letter, word, or passage.

But life doesn't always work out like it should, and during his teenage years, Moshe drifted away from studying the Bible and into studying science. Unlike in biblical studies, every day in science can bring the latest in new products or services. But perhaps just like Bible study, science may bring new meaning, too.

Early on, Moshe became interested in water purification in his role at the Weizmann Institute of Science in Israel. After earning his PhD, he joined a company called Hydranautics, which manufactured membranes for the desalinization of water. In the subsequent years, he continued to work on developing various methods of water purification. It was literally his life's calling. It gave him great meaning, just like biblical studies did all those years ago, as clean water is in dire need around the world.

The need to access clean drinking water has been at the heart of Moshe's life work because the statistics are, quite frankly, shocking:[2,3,4]

- Most waterborne infections are spread by the fecal–oral pathway, which happens when human feces are consumed by drinking contaminated water or eating tainted food. That ends up happening mostly through inadequate sewage management and sanitation.

- 1.8 million people die of a diarrheal disease (including cholera and others) every year. This unfortunately overwhelmingly impacts children, 90% of whom are under age five. 88% of these deaths are attributed to unsafe water supplies.

- It is anticipated that three billion people will experience water stress by 2025 due to limited access to clean water.

It was clear that something needed to be done. Then in 2002, everything changed. Moshe got a call from a Dutch company called Vestergaard Frandsen. They were looking for a superstar in the water purification world that would help bring the vision to life of a straw that could make any water safe to drink. The vision was nearly impossible: the straw was to have no moving parts, and it was supposed to run without electricity or any batteries. And it was to last for at least 700 liters (which is about a year of drinking water per person). And perhaps the most difficult wish list item? It was supposed to be cheap.

Perhaps Moshe's former rabbinical studies came in handy as his invention may have been assisted by divine intervention. For what he came up with changed the world forever.

Moshe and his business partners came up with a straw called LifeStraw. And this straw has literally enabled millions of people around the world to drink directly from water that is contaminated and otherwise unfit to drink. It has no moving parts, is not powered by a battery. It is easily held in one hand and weighs just a few ounces. It works just like any other straw would. You place the tip of the straw into a water source and, using suction, you pull water into your mouth. The filter inside is a disinfecting resin, developed and patented by Moshe, that captures contaminants in the tube of the straw before it reaches the mouth of the user. Its genius is in its simplicity. It literally has no start-up time or learning curve. You just put the straw into the water and drink.

Moshe said, "Around one-sixth of the world's population suffers from a shortage of clean drinking water. Every day, thousands die from waterborne diseases. My dream has been to help find a solution for those millions of people that are faced with this problem. Today, that dream is close to becoming a reality. About two million already use the water purification straws, and

I hope that in the near future, the tens of millions of people in countries that don't have access to clean drinking water will be able to benefit from them."[6]

The lack of clean drinking water is one of the biggest health crises we face. Not as a nation, or even a region, but as humanity. And this invention of a simple straw that is easy to carry and can enable a drink of water anytime, anywhere – one of the most basic necessities of humans – simply by the design of an ingenious filter, is a game changer.

The Five Stages of Boredom Grief

Moshe Frommer's LifeStraw invention and the company that now produces it got me thinking a lot about the use of filters in our everyday lives. Filters by their very nature are not a total block, like a dam on a river, they are made to allow certain things pass through while blocking out other things. So how do we decide what to let in and what to keep out? Experience.

Experience drives the decision point of what the filter should be doing in the first place. If we experience international hardships in access to clean water, then designing a filter to keep out the bad water and allow in the good water makes perfect sense. The most impressive part of this is that we can decide what types of filters to set up in our lives and how to use them, depending on what we want to keep and what we would like to discard.

At work, applying filters at the right time and in the right way can mean the difference between wild success and crushing failure. Sure, it's easy to envision the filter of keeping our mouth shut instead of saying what we want to say to that pesky coworker. That's an easy filter to apply at work. Just keep your mouth shut; if you can't, don't insult that pesky coworker with whatever you say. But filters like tolerance, acceptance, empathy, recognition, patience, understanding, hope, and others are far more difficult to implement at work. Just like choosing to filter our thoughts about that pesky coworker to create a more harmonious work life, most of us need that same game changer in our day-to-day lives – a filter to clean up our interactions, filter our initial reactions, and sometimes filter out our less desirable traits and boost the better ones in our careers.

But we are so bad at using filters at work on a day-to-day basis. We send that angry email only to regret it later; we eat up all our time being distracted and then complain that we don't have enough time to work; and finally we are busy making friends at work and building alliances, only to find out later that comes back to bite us in the ass. We will review several tools we can use later in this chapter, but for now it is sufficient to say that using filters can indeed be a superpower if we know how and when to use them to improve our creativity and innovation at work and beyond.

I have a favorite technique for demonstrating how filters work when I conduct keynotes across the country. When I am on stage, I tell the attendees that we are going to do a little exercise in the use of filters, and we will be filtering out one of the most common distractions around: our cell phones.

I ask all the audience members to put their phones away or turn them off. Usually there is an audible sigh because we are so attached to these devices. I also ask attendees at the conference to put away their laptop computers. To shut them down and put them away. When I look out to see if the conference attendees have followed my direction, I often see a few people – the laggards – taking forever to put their laptop or their mobile devices away, hoping that they can get out of doing this activity because it is that painful for them to be without a device. Scientists call this longing for our phones "attachment anxiety"[7] and have even studied the proximity effect of a phone being closer to the body as being a measure of comfort or discomfort, depending on the distance.

Then, I give the laggards some extra time. I'll say something like "I've got all day" and get a few chuckles while the laggards receive a bit of peer pressure to follow suit. I wait until most everyone in the room puts their phone and computers away. Note there has never been a time when everyone puts all devices away. It has never happened.

When I look out at the audience at this point, I usually see some deep irritation.

Next, I put a slide up on the projector or LED screen behind me that has a simple black dot, just a simple black dot in the middle of the screen.

Then, I ask the attendees to focus on the black dot on the screen, and I announce that we are about to conduct a study on the use of a filter to eliminate distractions. They can practice it at work when they feel there is just too much going on and they feel overwhelmed. I ask them to focus on the dot.

Now I see some further irritation on the face of most attendees. I tell the attendees that they don't really have to keep staring at the dot – and the only reason the dot is up there in the first place is because we are so bad at having nothing to do – being bored – that if I didn't have the dot up there, people wouldn't know what to do. (In earlier versions I had a black screen and people indeed did not know where to look. It was awkward, hence the dot.) I tell attendees that I will be setting a timer and that we are about to embark on a journey into the use of the distraction filter, which will filter out all distractions and allow only our creative and innovative thoughts to come though, a sort of mediation.

It is here when I start the timer that I can see – over the course of just a few minutes – what I like to call the Five Stages of Boredom Grief begin to take over. This is basically the five stages of grief, but this time the bereavement is over the momentary loss of their computer or cell phone! In the first few seconds, I see the first stage of boredom grief: denial. People around the room deny this is even happening. They are in shock that their phones are gone and their laptops are shut down. Next comes the second stage: anger. They are irritated and resentful that they were told to put their phone away. Next comes the third stage: bargaining. Attendees think if they just play along I will tell them they can open their phone or laptop in a bit, and this will be all over soon. After that is the fourth stage: depression. The audience in one way or another gets depressed and sad, literally sad. Finally, we reach the goal of the fifth stage: acceptance.

Acceptance comes at the two- or three-minute mark of my stopwatch. And I can tell something amazing is happening when attendees smile or talk to one another softly. All of this plays out in such a short time that when I ask attendees after the keynote how long the section on filters and distractions felt, they tell me it felt like half an hour. (It is only two or three minutes.)

Finally, I tell my audience that what they just experienced over the last few minutes is what I call the Five Stages of Boredom Grief, akin to bereavement. The pull of our technology is *that* strong, and we feel its loss *that* profoundly. But there is hope. Anytime we want, we can use filters to pick and choose what we want to let in and what we want keep out. Thankfully, most filters are easier to apply than filtering distractions. By going through the exercise and working through the Five Stages of Boredom Grief, attendees gain the power to implement these filters wherever they need them – in their work and beyond.

We are so used to plugging up every single minute of our free time with some distraction that we are seldom present any longer. We need to learn how to filter it out. If you don't believe me, go to a doctor's office and look at the waiting room. Each person is on their cell phones. Go on a plane ride. Same thing. Go to a sporting event – shockingly – same thing. People are not only using distraction to self-soothe[8] with their mobile phones – they are even distracted when there is something interesting going on – like a great keynote or a sporting event or concert.

But why are we so hesitant to put our phones down for a minute? Why are we so hesitant to use filters in our careers and embrace superpower #3 to enable deep creative and innovative thinking?

Hesitation to Use Filters

It seems that the lack of using filters in our lives at work and beyond is tied to choosing to look at situations in non-creative ways. We tend to gravitate toward what we cannot control instead of looking at what we can control. What I mean is that when given the opportunity to look at something that happens in our careers at work, we often choose to look at the situation in a way that is not creative, not imaginative, or not fully thought through. For example, take the way most of us look at our current jobs.

Most of us would say – and the research shows – that our current job is terrible[9] for whatever reason and that we would be thrilled to leave it for another job. The grass always appears greener on the other side. But when you do quit this job and take that job, are you much happier? Studies have shown that folks who quit one job to take another job are often disappointed in that new job – as it's not making them as happy as they thought it would.[10]

And here is where the filter concept comes in.

Instead of abandoning ship at your current job and calling it all terrible, I am willing to bet that there are meaningful parts of the job that you actually enjoy. Parts of the job that are fun or challenging and projects that you enjoy working on. So why not Use a Filter to filter out the bad parts of the job and instead focus on the good parts? If we learn how to Use a Filter to align our expectations, we may be way happier by looking at work in a creative way, instead of a non-creative way. Look at the "terrible" job that you have for whatever joy it brings you, focus on the positive aspects, not the negative aspects of the job. Filter your perception of the negative to allow the good of the job to overpower the bad or "terrible" parts of the job.

I am not saying that this filter superpower will work in all cases. It may be the case that your job is truly terrible and that you would be much happier working elsewhere. But here's the thing: everyone thinks that, and it is seldom the case. In fact, in one study, 72% of employees report "shift shock" – shifting from one job to another left them regretful.[11] Perhaps the work of self-reflection to really see if the grass is greener on the other side is worthwhile at this point, because you may be a serial job taker who bounces around every 18 months or so continually looking for a company where you may be happy. Other than strategic reasons for doing this, like getting a better salary or a higher position (which are worthwhile pursuits), bouncing around endlessly looking elsewhere for some mythical perfection won't make you happy. You will find that no company is perfect. No organization runs exactly the way you want it to run. But what you can control is your use of superpower #3 to filter how you feel about your current job, letting the good in and blocking out the bad.

Imagine being able to filter out the bad of your job and to focus on the good instead. Would that make you happier at work? You bet. I have been in leadership for most of my career; but it didn't start that way. Seldom does anyone start that way. Everyone at some point had to work their way up. And I spent many years grinding out at jobs that were less than ideal. And I blamed the job! It wasn't my fault. It was their fault. So I kept leaving each job to go to the next one and never found happiness or satisfaction at work until I discovered that I was not using superpower #3 to filter out the bad and keep the good. I expected the job or the marketplace to do that for me, and I was left disappointed when it didn't happen. But once I began to Use a Filter to sift out the bad and amplify the good, I found that I was much happier in the workplace. These days I help staff at the company I run understand that no job is ever perfect and that using a filter will help to properly balance their work lives so they too can find happiness and balance.

But it's not only at work that we tend to view things though a negative filter. It's our relationships too.

Let's look at the marriage statistics in the United States. At the time of this printing, the U.S. divorce rate is roughly 42%.[12] Every 42 seconds, there is a divorce in America. That means that just about half of all marriages end in a divorce. In the time it takes to undergo an average wedding reception, which is about 5 hours, 430 divorces happen across the United States!

Now some marriages are beyond repair, yet most people who seek divorce[13] use the same reasons: under-appreciation, lack of commitment, arguing too much, unrealistic expectations of each other, lack of equality in the relationship, jealousy, infidelity, and the like. Unsurprisingly, it turns out that some of the best data on divorce comes from divorce attorneys.[14] And when their clients are asked if they were at fault for the divorce, nearly all say that the other person is at fault. No matter what led to the divorce in the first place – it was always someone else's fault.

So, while Using a Filter may not save every marriage, what would happen if we were to look at marriage or even our friendships or work relationships through a filter? Let's choose the filter of tolerance here to look at our marriage. No marriage is perfect, but I wonder what would happen if the same 42% of people who do choose divorce would look at their marriage through a filter of tolerance. What would they see? Would they filter out some of the less desirable traits and allow in the more desirable ones? Instead of nitpicking everything that may be wrong, would they choose to look at what was right? What would happen to their marriage?

When we Use a Filter like tolerance to allow ourselves permission to focus on the positives of our spouse or friends, we just may be happier overall. It's a choice we can make to use superpower #3 in a way that allows us to adjust better to situations, instead of blaming others for fulfillment that we do not receive.

The best part of Using a Filter is that it is a choice. Let in the positive and filter out the negative like Moshe has done with dirty water. Now that is entirely possible and achievable in the world of work and beyond, and here are some must-have tools to help you choose your filters and tap into your creative and innovative mind. Let's jump in with the first tool, Send It Later.

Tool #1: Send It Later

We have all been there: you get a dreaded email from that irritating coworker who is just a drag, and you don't even want to open it. But you do open the email. Just reading the first sentence gives you that all-too-familiar ill feeling. You think to yourself what have I done wrong in a previous life to deserve working with this person – it's that bad. You feel your pulse elevate with each passing word you read. You get a tightening in your throat. Your blood begins to boil. Your first reaction as your eyes scan the email is to get defensive. Who does this person think they are! Why are they sending me this kind of email! Why does this always happen to me! So, you do what most of us do, and you hit Reply. Then you go scorched earth on this person in a rash and quick rebuttal. You hit Send. It's all over within seconds. It may have felt good five minutes ago, but now as you have calmed down you check your sent folder and think: oh no – what have I done? You read sentences that don't make sense, anger that is not characteristic of how you normally react, and a whole sense of regret starts to wash over you.

Don't worry. I've been there before. Everyone has. But there has got to be a better way.

The Send It Later tool starts by denying your first impulse. Filter it out as a first impulse because it is usually wrong. Often-times, we need a filter to prevent ourselves from reacting too quickly. Especially at work. Research has shown that our initial reactions can often be overly emotionally charged[15] and therefore unreliable. We are reactive animals after all, driven by impulse to survive. When we lived in caves and roamed from place to place in search of food, this impulsive trait was a welcome addition to keeping us alive. If we were threatened, we didn't need an hour break or time to process our feelings. We needed to act. Now! Back then, we didn't have the luxury of processing that something was going to kill us and eat us. That rash impulse – our ability to react right now – is what got us here today, to modernity.

But in modernity the usefulness of quick and rash impulse has become less and less valuable – and quite frankly undesirable – in the workplace.[16] Scientists call this impulse to react "discounting" in a very literally way – as if we are "discounting" our ability to think a problem all the way through diligently and take the time necessary to arrive at a thoughtful decision. Moreover, rash instinctual reactions at work have been shown to lead to a whole host of negative consequences – some even dangerous, leading to injury or disease because we act too fast without thinking things through. And we are led to take risks that often we wouldn't take if we were to just slow down instead.[17]

And this is not just for emails. It is for every kind of interaction you have at work. From a testy meeting to a less-than-civil interaction with a coworker or client, slowing down to Send It Later can be a useful tool to allow yourself time to think.

So tool #1 focuses on Using a Filter to keep your first reaction at work to a minimum – especially if that reaction is emotionally charged. If you are feeling overwhelmed, stressed, or otherwise under the gun, Send It Later can come in handy, especially when you feel you are pressed to react instantly. Here are some important things to remember:

- Most occurrences at work are not life and death – things can and should often wait. Not everything at work needs fixing right now.

- Ask yourself a few questions before you react to that email or occurrence – whatever it may be – to see if you still feel that way an hour later, or a day later. If you wait, the sting often subsides, and you can devise a more informed and strategic reaction better suited to the situation than your first instinct.

- If you feel pressed at a particular moment to react, say something like "let me get back to you" or "this is going to require some thought." We often feel that we need to have every answer at our fingertips, and often that is simply not the case.

- Don't be afraid of asking for time to process an idea, thought, email, meeting, client/vendor communication, and so on. It is okay to take your time and make a better decision after you have weighed all the factors than hurrying to make a rash decision in the moment no matter how much pressure you are under. Oftentimes coworkers and others will pressure you to make a decision based on mob rule hysteria – not what is really going on. People at work and beyond can get spun up quickly and feel that something is mission critical and needs to get dealt with now, now, now, when in fact, it can wait.

The perception of the heightened importance of a particular issue is often far larger than the actual need. The actual need may be to wait a few days to reply to the hostile email or wait an hour before replying to the client emergency or that new testy report from the meeting. But we are often so harried in our response that we lose the valuable and important creative spark that can occur when taking time to fully think something though before reacting. So, Send it Later.

Tool #2: Make More Time

What would you do if you knew you could have extra minutes added to your day? This is not some kind of sci-fi time machine or a time warp we enter to bend the fabric of space and time. It is literally a technique – a tool that anyone can use – to Make More Time. Because most people's average day looks something like this: You start off by checking emails and get a text to reply to something. So, you shoot off a text and, before you know it, you're in a meeting. Then an important email notification comes though on your computer, so you click it – in the middle of the meeting – to check what the email says. You reply to the email while you're still in a meeting and someone calls on you. A fire drill. There is something wrong with the order/client/company/you. You fumble some sort of answer to whatever question is asked of you on the phone, but you're only half listening, half thinking about the email you just sent no less than 30 seconds ago. Suddenly, another text hits your phone, followed by a phone call. You're still in that same meeting, but you step away and field that phone call, then rejoin the meeting and try to catch up. Then you notice that the meeting is finally over, and you repeat some variation of this for the next eight to ten hours at work, thinking that you have done a great job and were able to handle so many little fire drills all at once! But the day is a blur, and you can't remember the last time you were able to focus on anything at work to see it all the way through. Does this sound familiar? What if I were to tell you that this mental fog and constant assault on your cognition could be avoided?

In order to get time back into your day, you must stop multitasking.

Study[18] after study[19] has shown that multitasking is one of the worst things you can do to increase productivity, so as part of your filter superpower, I'd like to offer you the superpower of doing one thing and focusing on it until you complete it, before moving on to the next activity.

Instead of consistent distraction throughout your day, just focusing on one thing and completing it before you move to the next saves time. When you are working on one thing and something else pops up, forcing you to multitask, you lose time instead of gaining it. For example, if you are sending an email and someone chats you on Slack or some other messaging app, the time it takes to respond to the message and get back to what you are doing is significant. And it adds up, compounding with each distraction. Researcher Gloria Mark told *Fast Company* that her research has shown[20] that most people take over 23 minutes to refocus on whatever they were doing after just one interruption.

So to gain more time in your day, stop multitasking. Do one thing and finish it before moving onto the next. Resist the temptation that comes along with trying to do everything and anything at once, and you will find more clarity, better problem-solving abilities, and, best of all, a more creative and innovative approach to solving problems at work and beyond. When we multitask, we rob the ability of our brain to do what it was designed for. And what it was designed for is to pull all of our thoughts and ideas together – a cumulative approach to all our life's experiences – to be able to look at problems and solve them one at a time. We rob ourselves of that ability when we multitask, so Using a Filter to block out distraction is critical for engaging our brain in long-term problem-solving abilities. Also, when we multitask, we are no longer "present." We are no longer in the moment, able to solve problems in a specific time and place.

But you must be present in order to reap the rewards. You cannot let your mind drift off or quickly check that text you just got. You literally have to filter out distractions in order to implement this important tool and allow yourself the time you deserve to solve pressing issues and be present enough to enable your mind to solve them.

Tool #3: Don't Make Friends at Work

I know that recommending that you Don't Make Friends at Work may be a controversial topic. In fact, I have seen the controversy it can invoke. In June of 2023 I published an article in *Psychology Today*[21] that went viral. It was translated into several languages all over the world and was a top-viewed article.

The topic was about friends and the workplace, and I got several scathing emails and comments about it. In the article, I write about how making friends at work often distracts you from your goals, and, indeed, that you should focus on other things to deepen creativity and innovation at work.

Taking it a step further from where my article left off, I now believe that Using a Filter to block out a desire to make friends with our coworkers is essential. I believe now that making friends with your coworkers and others that you work with is one of the most critical mistakes that people make today at work, and that implementing a filter to separate your workplace coworkers from your friends – your true friends – is an essential component of becoming more creative at work and being able to solve problems with a Solution Mindset. Don't get me wrong. You need positive, effective, working relationships with coworkers so you can collaborate effectively as a team. Workplace relationships are important. But they shouldn't be tangled up with true friendships.

The reasons we should avoid friendships at work, and instead look to build networks and connectivity, are multiple.[22] One of the most important reasons we should avoid making friends at work is that work is not a social construct. There are many social constructs in our society that are better suited to making friends, like clubs, special interest groups, churches, synagogues, and more. These institutions are set up for social aspects, not for commerce.

The modern workplace exists not for the building of friendships but for the execution of commerce. And anything that detracts from that main goal gets in the way of solving problems and executing objectives. Friendships can also be very complicated to maintain at work. Who's in the in-group in a clique? Do you end up talking too much with someone socially instead of focusing on talking about the project with them? If you're friends with a coworker and a third colleague feels excluded, is your team working well? Do you avoid addressing workplace problems because you don't want to jeopardize a friendship? You shouldn't even start a business with your friends! The roadside is littered with stories of friends who have gone on to start a business together only to find that something ends up happening – usually some personal drama – and the venture is no longer intact due to some type of ego issue, a perceived slight, or other interpersonal offense.

Another problem with making friends at work is that the friendships are not of the same quality that you achieve when you separate commerce from genuine friendships. Sure, a coworker may seem like a bestie until she gets promoted and is now your boss. What do you do then? Yes – that vendor who provides you with a service may seem like a friend, but what happens when you have to switch to a different vendor for a price cut? When a work friendship goes sour, how do you continue to work well together after that? Not to mention dating at work.

Friendships are some of the most important relationships you will make in your life. And keeping them free and clear of commerce – Using a Filter to separate them from your workplace – can literally be one of the most important investments in your career. Companies will tell you that you are family and that everyone is friends with one another – but don't believe it. Companies fire people all the time. Families don't. Companies replace staff often. Friends don't.

So instead of looking to make friendships at work, look to boost your network. Networks are a collection of people you work with that you can help and can help you get to the next level. Everyone is on a different path; what may be your goal is not the same as someone else's goal. And having a solid network in place enables you to lend a hand to someone on a different path than yours and get a hand when you need it in exchange.

A shocking recent study discovered that only 11%[23] of employees consider their relationships with coworkers as one of the top factors contributing to their job satisfaction. *Only 11%.* For most people who think that their bestie is in the cube right next to them, that means other workplace aspects far outweigh their friendship. Other items like compensation, career growth, or management style hold more weight than friendships in determining overall job happiness.

Using tool #3 will enable a much greater joy at work – one where your friends are your friends, and your coworkers are your coworkers. Filtering out relationships that are truly based on merit and not on the conviviality of the workplace can be a game changer for embedding creativity and innovation in all you do.

Conclusion

In this chapter, we explored the third superpower – the ability to Use a Filter – to let desirable traits shine through while blocking harmful ones. We looked at amazing innovations like LifeStraw and how boredom is necessary for clarity and creativity. Now, we are going to look at another very important superpower that will continue the Use a Filter superpower. We will look at the fourth superpower, Take a Chance.

4

Superpower #4: Take a Chance

What Re-imagining Schools in Seychelles Teaches Us About Succeeding When the Odds Seem Insurmountable

A man of genius makes no mistakes. His errors are volitional and are the portals of discovery.

—James Joyce

The African continent has the youngest population on Earth.[1] That's a lot of kids who need an education. And it makes sense that quality schools should be a priority, but it's simply not the case. According to data on African education,[2] over one-fifth of kids between the ages of 6 and 11 are not attending school, while roughly a third of young people between 12 and 14 years old are not attending school. It gets worse. About 263 million children and youth are out of school, according to new data from the UNESCO Institute for Statistics.[3] The total includes 61 million children of elementary school age, 60 million of middle school age, and the first-ever estimate of those of high school age at 142 million.

That's a whole lot of kids missing out on one of the most basic of human dignities, that is, the ability to read, write, and at the most basic level, learn how to think for themselves. But there is hope. And that hope is extraordinary.

One glaring exception to the troubling stats above and a great hope of Africa is the nation of Seychelles. As you may remember from the introduction, Seychelles (pronounced: SAY SHELLZ) is a small archipelago country consisting of 115 islands in the Indian Ocean, off the coast of East Africa. Today, the statistics on education in that country are simply breathtaking:

- #1 ranked country for education in all of Africa.[4]

- One of the top 50 school systems anywhere in the world, ahead of Ukraine, Hungary, Russia, and the United Arab Emirates.[5]

- Enrollment rate for elementary school is 97%.[6]

- Ranked 28th in the world for teaching and critical thinking.[7]

Now, how in the world did Seychelles overcome huge challenges that other countries in Africa couldn't figure out? And how did they succeed when the odds seemed insurmountable? Seychelles took a chance, which is superpower #4. Using the Take a Chance superpower, Seychelles has transformed generations of kids, giving them a chance to succeed where one did not exist before. And learning how we too can use this superpower at work and beyond to Take a Chance on our initiatives, desires, and goals can kickstart that same mighty transformation.

In order to fully understand how profoundly the Take a Chance superpower has taken hold in Seychelles, we must look at the formative years that occurred between 1977 and 1998,[8] when a lot of chances were taken. Because at each turn of events, Seychelles decided to wager big by Taking a Chance on education. They took a chance by not being afraid to fail. And in doing so, they transformed their own failing educational system (which was on par with the rest of Africa) by using creativity and innovation to make it one of the most premier systems anywhere in the world. Here's how they did it:

- First, Seychelles took a chance on creating an educational vision where one did not exist before. The educational vision was bold – and a radical departure from what previously existed. Seychelles wanted to have the best public education system in all of Africa. Without any precedent, Seychelles' government took a chance on a directive to make education available for all, for life, and for personal and national development. It was sort of like a company charter where a company does not yet exist, but founders are Taking a Chance on their shared vision. Seychelles took a chance on a vision that was just that: a vision. And sometimes simply declaring intent is enough to get transformational change jumpstarted.

- Next, Seychelles changed policy in terms of parental involvement. They dictated that no students were permitted to miss school unless it was for a really good reason. If a child failed or neglected to regularly attend school without a good reason, each of their parents was liable to receive a significant monetary fine and three months imprisonment. Talk about getting serious about education! They took a chance on the gamble that if they got parents involved early and with consequence, parents would ensure their kids showed up at school. This was simply Taking a Chance on new ideas and trying to execute them in real life. No roadmap, no recipe to follow, just the sheer will to Take a Chance and mend a broken educational system.

- Then, Seychelles started on infrastructure with existing school renovations and new school construction. They took a chance on building the infrastructure before almost anything else was in place. By 1982, 71 new schools, 15 science laboratories, and 37 pre-schools were opened.

- With the facilities in place, they now turned to teachers. They took a chance on what they called "supply teachers," which are teachers with no teaching qualifications, and armed them with lesson plans and incentives. These incentives were geared at moving "supply teachers" to become more educated teachers. Eventually, in 1988, Seychelles saw an over 600% increase in teachers that were fresh college graduates. They made teaching an attractive career by enabling proper funding and also – perhaps most importantly – endless revisions of approach, lesson plans, and the efficacy of teaching. They left no stone unturned as they continually changed classroom teaching to keep up with new trends and emerging themes. This led to empowering teachers to continually modify and adapt, making the profession rely heavily on a Solution Mindset to increase student outcomes.

Today, Seychelles stands as a beacon of education – not just for Africa, but for the world – built on a simple yet powerful tenet: what if we dared to Take a Chance?

Flexibility versus Rigidity

One of the most impressive accomplishments from the Seychelles public school system is not a statistic that shows up on a spreadsheet, the bottom line, or in the data. But it is one of the most important components of Seychelles' Take a Chance superpower. It is the power of embracing continual revisions and quickly and actively adapting based on the results on the ground.

When we Take a Chance on our idea, we often feel the gravity and seriousness of the decision. And immediately we begin to question whether it was the right decision to make. What if we get it wrong? What if another idea was a better idea to Take a Chance on? But if we couple the Take a Chance superpower with the ability to adapt and adjust on the ground as results come in, we fully embrace the transformative power of Taking a Chance and the benefits it can bring us.

Being able to set a plan in motion and continually adjusting to make sure that the plan can adapt to the realities of what is going on in real time is critical to the success of Taking a Chance. Most companies that Take a Chance on an idea fail because the idea is too rigid, too locked into an implementation that is unchangeable. When using the Take a Chance superpower, allowing the implementation to adapt and not be static will enable the vision to fit the reality of the market forces that act upon that idea, and shape it to maximize the chances of success.

For example, Seychelles had gotten rid of private schools early on in their implementation of the vision of having the best public schools. They figured that narrowing down the options for parents to one choice only for schools would ensure attendance and engagement. But what they found along the way was that parents wanted a choice in where they sent their kids to school, and so they adapted, adjusted, and changed the implementation to allow for private schools. The adaptability away from a rigid construct and into a malleable assembly of the vision ensured that the goal was attainable even if the path to attainability wasn't preordained. Be flexible. Adapt to the latest.

One of the more predictable mistakes I see when consulting with companies on the implementation of the fourth superpower is that companies usually have a pretty good idea of what it is that they want to Take a Chance on. And they implement that initiative with an iron fist, without allowing for deviations on the pathway to achieving that goal. The hesitancy to allow for deviations is born out of a fear that any path away from the "correct one" will result in a watered-down goal or even perhaps a changed goal. So the logic follows that rigid control of the implementation is critical.

But one of the things that I argue in my work that may seem counterintuitive is that the pathway to implementing the Take a Chance superpower is less attractive than setting the goal in the first place. Whether the goal is to make Seychelles the best educational system in the world, or to be promoted to supervisor by the end of the year, or to increase sales for the southwest franchise stores, the goal in and of itself is important. The pathway to get to that goal is far less so. And here is where it gets interesting: the path to that goal needs to stay flexible as solutions to individual roadblocks along the way need to be customized per each application. And that is okay. It is better than okay – it's the entire point.

Seychelles, for example, could have collapsed their vision many times as roadblocks no one initially thought of kept popping up along the path of implementation, threatening to derail the whole thing. For instance, there was a national movement to embed patriotism in upper age ranges of kids as part of the curriculum that failed spectacularly. But instead of scrapping the whole vision like most people would do at the first sight of problems – they simply changed the curriculum and kept the target goal of making the public school system the best in Africa the same. A steadfast commitment to keep changing the pathway to the goal, yet not changing the goal itself, is desirable in implementing superpower #4, Take a Chance. So in this case, patriotism classes out, goal still intact.

When Taking a Chance on an idea, keeping as flexible as possible when you implement doesn't dilute your goal – it enables the highest chance of its coming to fruition. As we Take a Chance on some of our ideas – no matter what they are – we must also allow for a fluid path to realize the goal. Yet often we are afraid of Taking a Chance on our ideas in the first place.

Embrace Your Eudaimonia

Taking a Chance on an idea is difficult for us in general because it involves practicing some self-regulation over our emotions and our behaviors. We want to be passionate about Taking a Chance, but sometimes that same passion can overtake reason and lead us to make bad decisions. We want to be strong when Taking a Chance, but sometimes that same strength takes us away from our goal because we become inflexible. We want to be smart about Taking a Chance, but sometimes that same knowledge leads us to alienate supporters with elitism. Studies have shown that overcoming theoretical boundaries[9] – boundaries that are there because we imagine them to be there – are among the most difficult to overcome. Especially at work.

It is difficult to Take a Chance on an idea because we feel that the idea may not be a good one in the first place. Or we think we may not have enough resources to pull the trigger. In the example of the school system in Seychelles, they took remarkable risks by Taking a Chance on their vision: building infrastructure and spending real money without knowing if the vision would work out or not. That seems risky to us.

And we are overwhelmingly a risk-averse society, which has been shown[10] to reduce creativity and innovation by maintaining the status quo. Instead of Taking a Chance, we usually do the opposite. Yet the important thing to remember when using superpower #4 is what would happen if we were *not* to use the superpower. What if we were *not* to Take a Chance on our ideas and see how far they could take us? The risks of Taking a Chance are there for sure – but the risks of not Taking a Chance? Far greater.

Scientists have a term called *Eudaimonia* (pronounced: YOU DAI MONI AH). It's a Greek word that translates roughly to "good spirit" or "flourishing" especially when used to describe our own ambitions, ideas, well-being, and meaning in our lives. It is a state of good cheer, good spirit, and happiness that we tend to seek out in our day-to-day lives. And studies[11] have shown that Eudaimonia increases when we are faced with challenges in undertaking an initiative. Taken a step further, we can deduce that Eudaimonia can increase when we use superpower #4 and Take a Chance because we are activating something that has been very important to humans for millennia: meaning in our lives.

When we are able to cultivate meaning by Taking a Chance on an idea or concept that we want to bring into the world – no matter how large, like fixing schools in an entire country, or how small, like fixing a leaky sink – we tend to be better off for doing it. Our well-being – our Eudaimonia – is increased by taking on the act. So, no matter how hard it may be, not Taking a Chance will likely cause greater damage as it moves us away from a place of meaning. Research shows that human beings are "hardwired for meaning"[12] – and by not Taking a Chance we are denying this pursuit of meaning, which can take away intrinsic human programming – in other words, what we are meant to do in our lives. That meaning is specific to each person who takes a chance on an idea, because the meaning derived from such activity is as unique as you are.

Diving further into this idea of Eudaimonia, researchers have shown that meaningful work is all about what we personally view as significant. We can easily say that the school system in Seychelles is a significant meaningful venture – that is easy – but is it okay to say that our work to get a raise, expand to a new market, or even to have a great presentation at the board meeting is a significant venture – one that gives us meaning? Scientists say resoundingly: yes.[13]

Therefore, giving ourselves the permission to seek Eudaimonia by Taking a Chance becomes a critical component of what has potential to give us meaning in our day-to-day work and beyond. Yet we are afraid still, we don't really know how to Take a Chance, and we feel that we may fail. So, get ready to dive in with the first tool that anyone can use to help build that Eudaimonia and Take a Chance on ideas that could lead to the most significant creation in your life.

Tool #1: Fail on Purpose

People are afraid to fail, and this fear is a huge roadblock to creative problem-solving. There are so many potential fears people have when it comes to failing. Here are a few, and I'm sure you likely have your own to add:

- We worry that, when we fail, people will think we are stupid.
- We worry that people won't trust our next idea.
- We worry that our failure would be colossal.
- We worry about the worst-case scenario, that we might fail and lose our job or business.

These kinds of fear can freeze our minds, making it almost impossible to unlock ideas. Scientists[14] call this freeze *rumination*, and what that means is that we build up all this fear of failure at work and then repeatedly think about negative feelings, distress, and their causes and consequences over and over until we are forced into inaction. We cannot Take a Chance on our idea because we cannot focus on the potential success – the potential meaning and Eudaimonia we may receive from this venture – because we are stuck in a cycle of rumination. We stress and worry about failure. And that fear of failure can lead to not Taking a Chance on our ideas, which leads to a lack of the happiness and meaning that are right there at our fingertips, if we could just set aside our fear and reach out.

We need something to help us get used to failing and failure. Because once we experience it on a regular basis, it becomes easier to deal with, and we ultimately find out that it's not as bad as we may have thought – and indeed it is something we can surmount on our way to Taking a Chance to fulfill meaning in our lives. What if we practice failing so we get more comfortable at it? Like with any life skill, the more we practice, the easier it becomes.

No one was born with knowledge of how to ride a bicycle. Neuroscience[15] has shown that this is indeed the case, that the fear of failure endured when learning how to ride a bike was built into a pattern of procedural memory. And what that basically means is that learning how to ride a bike is a process consisting of patterns of failure that amount to a step-by-step process that eventually leads to success. And neurologically speaking, the brain remembers the failures and remembers how to build upon them to fulfill the goal of finally riding a bike.

You learn by failing a number of times until you get comfortable at it – and then it is a skill you keep for the rest of your life.

Learning how to fail properly can be a rewarding and enlightening tool – and that is exactly what this tool aims to do.

My Fail on Purpose tool in the Take a Chance superpower is all about that: Failing on Purpose. Now that may seem like counterintuitive advice or something that is simply rash or not fully thought out, but it is indeed a significant part of learning how to Take a Chance on your ideas and letting go.

Here is how it works.

Purposefully make mistakes in your everyday work to see that these mistakes that you make – on purpose – are not so bad. You will quickly see that indeed you will not get fired or that your rumination will not lead to catastrophic incidents. Now how you make those mistakes is very important. This is not about making mistakes in safety protocol or throwing all caution to the wind. This is about making calculated mistakes on purpose that show you how to get comfortable with error – just like learning how to ride a bike – in a way that the small errors build up to a foundation of learning that catapult you into the creative and innovative problem-solving superpower of Taking a Chance. This is about a deliberate error that is made not with the intention of carelessness or malice, but with the intention to learn, test boundaries, and spark creativity. Here is how you do it:

- Let's say for example that the majority of your day centers around email. Most of our work lives have become quite email centric, so there is a pretty good chance that this example applies to you. What you do to Fail on Purpose, and by extension learn how to Take a Chance on an idea, is to make an error in your email. Put a typo in the email. On purpose. Take a guess on something that you have been wanting to guess about but cannot for fear of failing. Remember it's all about the intention – so intend to push a boundary or intend to see if this mistake can lead to something worthwhile. Chances are that the email typo – or calculated guess – can spark some creativity and understanding that would have never been there in the first place if you didn't make the error. I remember many years ago, I intentionally added an extra zero on the left side of the decimal in a sales projection slideshow. There were a lot of nervous laughs at first, but soon someone in the room said, "Why not? – Why should we not try to hit that target?" A healthy, fun, and unexpected debate occurred among the sales team with some pretty good ideas on how to actually achieve that goal. The intentional mistake was not met with getting fired or some other out-of-control rumination. Sure, it was a bit uncomfortable for a few moments when the mistake was discovered at the presentation – but ultimately it led to a pretty healthy debate, which not only made the mistake worthwhile, but also enriched the discourse among team members.

• Another way you can purposefully make mistakes is to say something ridiculous in a meeting. We are all – no matter what we do – in meetings pretty much all day. And if not all day then at some point in our week we will find ourselves in a meeting. So intentionally make a mistake by blurting out something in a meeting that you know may be a mistake up front. You will see that the worst that can happen is not as bad as you expect. You may also see that this intentional mistake may open up doors that have been closed because the mistake frees up others to make mistakes too. And when we show vulnerability by allowing ourselves to make intentional mistakes, later when the mistakes are made naturally and unintentionally, our ability to not only deal with them but to thrive off them increases exponentially. It really is about making lemonade out of lemons, but we need to practice making lemonade because there are a ton of ways to do it. Be it sweetened, unsweetened, with a dash of ice tea, and so on – there are a ton of ways to take what you blurted out on purpose and craft it as a novel idea. Getting in the habit of making intentional mistakes will help us realize our mistake potential and enable us to Take a Chance on ideas.

Practice making mistakes and Failing on Purpose so that when failure occurs next (not a matter of if, but a matter of when), it will be much easier to deal with and far, far less scary.

Tool #2: Give 'Em a Chance

The business news talks constantly about a talent shortage like it is some existential threat that is imminently about to destroy every business across America. No matter where the news comes from, the narrative is mostly along these lines: there is no one good to hire and schools are not producing good talent and it's near impossible to find a good fit. In my own consulting, I constantly hear managers and HR professionals talk about how they can't find the right people for the open roles they have. But many of these same companies have hundreds, if not thousands of employees who, if given a chance, could take on these new roles successfully. And thrive.

One of the most famous sayings in the English language deals with the perception that the grass is always greener on the other side, and this tool deals with helping you see that the grass is not always greener on the other side. Furthermore, sometimes the best people to hire are right there all along, not some imagined or abstract people you are trying to find somewhere else. But we cannot seem to see them. So, after many years of keynotes and consulting and hearing the same thing repeatedly about the absence of talent across corporate America, I set out to find the truth. And it turns out that neuroscience has a lot to do with our inability to use tool #2, which is to Give 'Em a Chance to do the job.

The research has taken me on a journey to understand why hiring managers, HR professionals, and other leaders almost always look outside their organization for deliverance of top talent. And what I found is a syndrome in psychology called *focusing illusion*.

Humans make judgment calls of all kinds, from what to eat to who to marry, by using a subset of data instead of using all the available data. Selecting some data and throwing away the rest. Why do we do this? It's because we are wired to do so. The human brain is only wired to consider three to five options at a time. Three to five data points of consideration to weigh the pros and cons.[16] Look at what you had for breakfast this week. Think about what you had each day. It is entirely likely that it's three to five things that you usually or almost always eat, and rarely do you go outside of those limited choices. We give that subset of data, in this case our breakfast choices, more weight than we should. We like it. We will even try to defend it by saying that it's easy to eat what we ate or that it gives us energy to get through the day, or we may even say that it's fast and gets us out the door quicker. No matter what it is, that limited subset of data becomes familiar like a favorite pair of jeans. This limited data becomes an anchor for all subsequent decisions, and we focus on analyzing that subset of data before allowing anything else.

So, in the case of hiring managers and other leaders, they are used to hiring outside the company when looking for new talent. That is what is comfortable for us. This is why hiring managers and HR folks and leaders tend to view internal promotion "hires" with skepticism and external, unknown hires as superior. We need to get hiring managers and HR folks and leaders to eat a different breakfast. And that starts with Give 'Em a Chance.

More than likely there are some great people who you work with who if given a chance, would shine in a new role. Even if you are not the manager or HR professional, being able to recognize coworkers in the same light is valuable for your career. Because everyone loves a well-made team – and your ability to find strengths in coworkers to develop well-functioning teams is just as important as hiring in the first place.

Yet, sadly, most companies aren't open to moving people across job functions, like from product development to sales or from customer service to marketing. It takes too long to upskill people, and they make so many mistakes along the learning curve. But these frequently made arguments are precisely my point. The mistakes made along the way by these individuals that are promoted from within instead of hired from without are important. Because bringing in fresh perspectives allows you to learn from the failures of these individuals. What they do wrong may help pinpoint problems in your process that, if fixed, could open the door for creative problem solving.

The added bonus of promoting from within is that folks can apply knowledge management systems creatively by utilizing their experience in a different role in new ways in their new position. So if you are in leadership, Give 'Em a Chance is an incredible tool to use that bucks human psychology and allows for options outside the small data subset we love so dearly to have a chance to work and inject creativity into the process. And if you are on the front line, using Give 'Em a Chance will help you pull back from judgment and allow you to instead focus on the positive qualities of your coworkers.

Tool #3: Recognize Mistakes and Then Success

We live in a society obsessed with success. And that success seems to be measured in wins only. Everybody's moving at breakneck speed right now. We're on planes, meeting with clients, digging out of our inbox. It's 24/7/365 go time. Therefore, we don't have the time to recognize people when they're doing well, much less celebrate failed risk-taking. Yet celebrating failed risk-taking allows for success in ways we have never taken the time to fully understand. Until now. Success that is all around us may appear easy or natural, yet takes many years to develop into meaningful success because the very foundation of the success was built upon mistakes.

Take Sarah Blakely, founder of Spanx and Sneex, for instance. Her companies are now worth more than $1.7 billion,[17] but the road to get there wasn't easy or natural. She failed time and time again, at first as a Disney World employee and then a fax machine saleswoman. Yet each mistake led her closer and closer to success. Or take Mr. Beast of YouTube fame. Most people think that he uploaded a video one day and had instant success. But that is not the case. He uploaded videos for five long years with virtually no views or followers and made tons of mistakes before finally gaining traction as one of the world's most successful YouTubers, earning an estimated $1.4 billion dollars a year.[18]

Recognizing success is important – but recognizing mistakes and failure, then building on them is more important. Because very rarely is success had instantly, and the overwhelming majority of the time success comes from building upon mistake after mistake until you are on a path to success.

And all too often, mistake recognition comes too late. I encourage recognition to come earlier, at the precipice of a breakthrough, to encourage someone to keep going and take those final steps. They are just about almost there! And it is at this point the reinforcement is most needed – not after the breakthrough, when it is a mere acknowledgment, too late for the realm of support. I like to make an analogy here to climbing

Mt. Everest all the way up to its cloudy, poor-visibility summit. Imagine someone who climbs the mountain only to give up a few yards short of the summit because they can't see that they are almost at the top! It is here that they need that last bit of encouragement. But they often don't get it. So instead, they turn around to return back down the mountain, never knowing just how close they may have come to breaking through to the summit.

Our business world is the same. We too often quit so very close to reaching our goals that we never realize just how close we almost came to success. And we give up just short of reaching our own summit of Mt. Everest. There has got to be a better way, and tool #3 deals with encouragement at the least likely point: when making mistakes on the path to success.

So how do you do this? We start by looking at our own goals and accomplishments in the workplace and breaking up so-called "traditional success" goal accomplishment – which states that only when a goal is reached is it worth encouraging – and instead encourage mistakes. Traditional success views a goal as not grasped until the goal is fully accomplished. There is no half-way point or intermediary.

But why not?

Why shouldn't there be a midpoint or milestones along the path that encourages you to keep going? When looking at our own goals creatively, we need to insert some mile markers along the way to help us realize that we are indeed on the correct path. For instance, if you are trying to get a promotion at work as your goal, you can creatively break that path up into milestones to allow yourself to make little wins from all the mistakes you make along the way. That big meeting with the client that came after a few botched attempts? A milestone. That kind email from leadership after the client complained about a mistake that you fixed? A milestone. These milestones soon add up to a promotion, and all along the way you are recognizing the failures it took you to get there instead of beating yourself up at every mistake or failure. As soon as you recognize mistakes in yourself, you can move on to helping others recognize the value of their mistakes, too.

Start by looking at initiatives in a new and creative way. Sure, it's easy to look at a big quantifiable goal – for instance, if someone on the team made a big sale, it's easy to point out their great work. But what if a new client-outreach program only brought in two new clients? What do you do then? That's where the real magic begins for tool #3: Recognize Mistakes and Then Success. Because you have a choice of how you look at that perceived mistake, you can choose to look at it as a failure, or you can choose to mine it for all the success others cannot see. What may appear on a spreadsheet as a loss may just be the kernel of hope to launch upon an empire. Most people will see the hours that went into marketing to attract those new clients, the effort of time and treasure spent on positioning and strategy, only to come up short. And here we can decide, uncommonly and with a Solution Mindset, that's still two new clients you didn't have before – and perhaps this new idea just needs some adjustment.

Adjusting the idea based on what worked instead of what didn't work is the key differentiator. While most would quit, folks with a Solution Mindset would see opportunities where others see failure. What was it that attracted these two new clients? It is worth following up with them? Is it worth diving in deep to see what ended up working instead of looking at what failed? Did they receive the message you were putting out in a different way than the others? Recognizing mistakes and then looking toward success allows you to see what others may miss – and there is some value in every effort that can lead to an adjustment of some sort on the road to success.

The one-hit wonders litter the side of the road on the way to entrepreneurial achievement. They are everywhere. But sustainability in a chaotic world often forces us to Take a Chance on ideas that others may not Take a Chance on, and recognize mistakes and learn to build on them before giving up just short of the summit of our own Mt. Everest.

Conclusion

In this chapter we learned about the fourth superpower and all the ways to Take a Chance on our ideas. We looked at amazing chance-taking like the schools in Seychelles and how Eudaimonia thrives when we Take a Chance on our ideas and get creative. Now, we are going to examine another very important superpower that will continue the Take a Chance superpower. We see how the fifth superpower, Untangle Complexity, may just help us clear all the clutter and focus on simplicity with a solution, forever enabling us to solve problems big and small. Let's dive in.

CHAPTER

5

Superpower #5: Untangle Complexity

What Health Insurance in Japan Teaches Us
About Solving Problems with Simplicity

Ideas that enter the mind are simple. And unmixed.

—John Locke

It is difficult to imagine a transition more profound than how the Japanese people transformed following World War II. Japan's fundamental change from a wartime aggressor aligned with Nazi Germany and fascist Italy as part of the Axis of World War II[1] into a modern country replete with a new constitution, democratically elected officials, and economic ingenuity, is nothing short of a miracle.

But it didn't start that way.

In December 1941, Japan surprised the world with a shock attack on Pearl Harbor, pulling the US into the war.[2] Meanwhile, Japan's war machine committed more unspeakable atrocities, especially on women[3] and horrific "scientific" experiments[4] until almost four years later, in 1945, when the US dropped two atomic bombs on Japan bringing an end to the war.[5] Soon afterward General Douglas MacArthur[6] led a seven-year occupation of the Japanese Islands to help stop the spread of communism and to rebuild the country.

The US-led rebirth of Japan relied on some profound lessons learned from mistakes in nation building after World War I. Instead of saddling the country with debt, the US gave Japan financial assistance to the tune of over $3.5 billion dollars in today's money.[7] The US then helped Japan establish a new constitution – one that gave citizens a bill of rights, individual freedoms, and a parliamentary government.[8] Finally, in the late 1940s, the US launched what was known as the "Reverse Course,"[9] which was an economic program shifting away from demilitarization and toward building a democracy, developing an economic powerhouse and shift in national identity[10] inside the country.

The resilience of Japan's people, their ability to adapt and reconstruct their war-torn country into what it stands for today is one of the best success stories of modern nation building the world has ever known. And out of that incredible transformation comes a success story that is the envy of the world: Japan's healthcare system.

Consistently ranked among the top three healthcare countries around the world,[11] Japan offers excellent access to services required to sustain good health, including healthcare outcomes, healthcare infrastructure, disease density in the population, risk factors, and mortality rates. Across all these factors and more, Japan's consistently high ranking in healthcare started in the late 1950s as the nation developed into a global economic power, ultimately reaching universal healthcare coverage for all its citizens by 1960.[12]

Japan managed to do this and so much more by navigating one of the most complex systems in modernity, which is healthcare. Few nations get their healthcare right. The United States, for instance, ranks 69th in the world, lower than Seychelles, which comes in at 39th, and Slovenia, which comes in at 24th. Why is it so bad in the US?

In one word: complexity.

In the US, access to healthcare is complicated. Complexity is a choice, in this case made by providers, insurance companies, and the government. The complexity reigns unchecked. Healthcare in the US is limited for many people, which prevents folks from getting an early diagnosis on a health issue. Then, the insurance system is very, very complex – involving pre-approvals and specialists and scans that are not easily obtainable under the tangle of overwhelming convolution. Finally, the costs are eye watering.

The US spends more per capita on healthcare than any other nation on Earth.[13,14] Think about that for a moment. More than any other country. Where does all this money go? The spending generally goes to extremely high administrative costs, expensive prescription drugs, and a fragmented and horribly complex insurance system. And the most salacious part is this: the patient outcomes are not improved, which is the whole point of spending that much money in the first place!

Frustration sets in for Americans. A *JAMA* (*Journal of American Medical Association*) study, one of the most prestigious and influential medical journals globally,[15] released a study in 2023 titled, "Complexity in the US Health Care System Is the Enemy of Access and Affordability." That study relating complexity as an enemy of healthcare is one of the most cited research studies in *JAMA*'s history.[16]

This makes it all the more remarkable that Japan's healthcare system spends half the amount on patient outcomes[17] and sees much better results.[18] This got me thinking a lot about healthcare in general, but this research led me to think about what we can learn from what Japan is doing. What can we do that they are doing to spend less and get more? Can we apply this concept outside of healthcare? The tantalizing opportunities here to spend less and get more left me captivated. So, I had to learn more.

It turns out that the core of everything they do in the Japanese healthcare system is anchored in simplicity.

Instead of burdensome bureaucracy, they aim to simplify the process of healthcare at every turn. For instance, everyone is covered. No matter how old you are or how much you make, everyone has medical coverage. Then there is emphasis on early detection, which saves a ton of money in the long run and further simplifies the treatment as it's often far simpler to treat something upfront than to wait and treat lengthy, long-standing, compounding, festering issues.

The one thing that Japan does to simplify the process of medicine, which stands heads and shoulders above all the rest, is set a single fee for every incidence.[19] It's a stroke of simplicity genius. A fee schedule for healthcare is kind of like a menu at a restaurant; the prices for each and every "order," or in this case incident, are fixed. The fee schedule is then adjusted every two years to keep up with the latest changes and adjustments in healthcare. What that ultimately means is that, if you happen to slip on the floor and break your arm, no matter where you go to treat your broken arm, the cost is the same. From the fancy hospital to the rural one – the treatment, cast, medicine, physical therapy, and all other related care is the same, no matter where you go.

It's simple. It's easy to understand. Japan's healthcare system is the essence of superpower #5, which is to Untangle

Complexity and make it simple, to cut away the clutter and make things accessible, easy, and straightforward. And somehow all this healthcare-related simplicity got me thinking a lot about a juicy, flavorful cheeseburger.

Fast Food Done Simply

In-N-Out Burger was established in Baldwin Park, a bedroom community outside of Los Angeles in 1948. Much like Japan's post-war economic gains, the US was going through incredibly fast changes as the greatest generation was coming home from the war and establishing businesses in the post-war boom. One such business founded by Harry and Esther Snyder was dedicated to simplicity.

Harry and Esther knew that customers wanted their food quickly and easily. Harry was fond of saying, "Keep it simple. Do one thing. And do it the best you can."[20] Again, complexity is a choice, and unlike healthcare in the US, Harry and Esther made a decision to chase simplicity at every turn.

Coincidentally, around the same time, car culture was becoming a big deal in Los Angeles and other cities as the newfound affordability of the automobile found its way to just about every driveway.[21] And the car wasn't just transportation: it was a cultural icon. Hot-rod culture, racing, and cruising up and down Main Street were becoming popular in the US. And the car became a reflection of the owner: their style, their values, their essence. People loved their cars (and still do!). Add the fact that it hardly ever rains in Southern California, and you have a supreme combination of car culture and food.

This led to an unbeatable proposition from In-N-Out Burger: combine the love of the automobile with the love of a great meal.

But there was just one catch: at In-N-Out, you had to get out of your car to order your burger and fries. Other restaurants had "carhops," which were kids on roller-skates that would come to your parking spot and take your order before disappearing back into the kitchen. There was still a considerable wait involved before your food came back, so that was inefficient. The business of In-N-Out Burger was built around simplicity, so carhops wouldn't work.

Then, In-N-Out Burger tried to knock out a window in their kitchen to allow drivers to order directly from the cook.[22] But that proved clunky as well. The orders would require cooks to execute several different orders with a car beside the window that may or may not be the recipient of one. It was a mess. The cars backed up. The parking lot turned into a log jam. There had to be a way to untangle all this complexity and solve this pressing issue with simplicity.

Harry was a Navy vet and was forever tinkering with electronics. He was inspired by intercoms used on military ships during WWII and spent many nights after work in his garage trying to figure out how to simplify the ordering process so that his cooks did not have to multitask and could focus on one organized system.[23] And what he devised changed fast food forever.

He came up with the two-way speaker system that we are all familiar with today. The menu was in a huge, lit-up enclosure where drivers could pull up and speak into a microphone to communicate their order to someone in the kitchen. Then they would pull up to the window and collect their order, never having to step out of the car.

This dedication to simplicity is ubiquitous today, yet at the time it was novel. McDonald's didn't have drive thru's till the mid-1970s,[24] and Harry realized that to execute orders quickly, with quality and a dedication to simplicity, he had to limit the menu. He decided to focus on quality over quantity, sourcing the best ingredients from local farms and meat producers, most of which are the same purveyors In-N-Out Burger uses to this day, more than 70 years later.

The In-N-Out Burger menu in 1950 looked like this:

- Cheeseburger
- Hamburger
- French Fries
- Beverages/Soda
- Shakes

Today, the menu looks like this:

- Double-Double
- Hamburger
- French Fries
- Beverages/Soda/Hot Chocolate
- Shakes

Not much has changed at all in over 70 years. The Double-Double is pretty much just two cheeseburger patties in one burger. Except for hot chocolate, which they did experiment with in the 1950s and later brought back as a mainstay, just about all the changes at In-N-Out Burger have been beverage changes. The business is still fiercely family owned and run today by Harry and Esther's granddaughter Lynsi Snyder,[25] and every location is a company location, not franchised. This consistency in the dedication to simplicity has led to a cult following for their food, and people from all over the world make pilgrimages to eat at their restaurants. To this day, In-N-Out Burger maintains a dedication to simplicity in everything they do. And the cult-like following is still going strong today, over 70 years later.

The Weaponization of Complexity

Most people make things too complicated. Researchers have a name for this: *complexity bias*. It seems that we tend to make complex choices instead of making simpler ones when tasked with unraveling problems.

A group of researchers[26] recently sought to test whether people choose simple or complicated solutions when offered the chance to solve a problem. They devised several experiments and tested thousands of people.[27] Examples of their experiments were things like modifying a Lego structure, wherein adding a Lego costs money and taking away Legos was free. In another experiment, they devised a multicolored digital grid pattern, where participants needed to make the grid a uniform color. In all the experiments, the subtractive choice was the correct solution. In other words, making things simpler was the right choice.

So, what happened? It turns out that we are horrible at simplicity. In most of the various experiments, people failed to choose the simple solution at least 75% of the time. Some of the experiments showed people failing to choose the simple path to problem-solving a whopping 90% of the time! The experiments were met with tons of hand-wringing and overshot solutions that made the problem-solving tedious, overwhelming, and tiresome. And most of all, it made problem-solving far more complex than it needed to be. The study concluded by finding that the complexity bias toward "more is better" could explain things like the healthcare system in the US or other overly bureaucratic constructs.

So why do we automatically perceive that more is better or that we need to continually add something to solve problems at work?

It turns out that adding complexity often gives us a feeling of power at work. And this feeling of power is a destructive influence in our modern workforce, both in our careers and businesses. We all know a person at the office who always ends up making things far more complicated than they need to be – simply to ensure that they are the only ones who hold the key to solving that problem as a power play. Think about a department that always complicates things so that their mistakes go unnoticed under the cloak of obstacles and complexity. And finally, we have all dealt with the organizations who seem to be in the business of misdirection, deflection, and pointing fingers away from simplicity and into a world of complexity for their own gain.

This addition of complexity and the paradox of "more is better" is hardwired into us from our ancient ancestors.[28] It seems that, throughout human history, the scarcity of resources that were available or even obtainable was a constant threat to our very survival. We couldn't get enough calories from the hunt. We couldn't get enough heat to warm us through the endless winter nights. But there were always a few times when people were able to obtain the extra meat or the bigger fire, and those who consistently managed to get more lived longer. Therefore, this instinct to horde resources was useful to ensure that we and our offspring had the best chance for survival.

Yet today that same abundance that may have given our ancestors the chance to survive is more of a status symbol and a power play at work. The weaponization of complexity has become an apparatus used to derail simplicity because it provides a nefarious advantage for those who weaponize it. Yet we can make a choice – each and every day – to reject complexity and choose simplicity by not weaponizing complexity for our own gains, and by embracing simplicity for a wider benefit.

And perhaps the best part of simplicity is that it has been shown to be good for business in study[29] after study.[30] So how do you knock away this tendency to complicate things? How can you make choices to be more like Esther and Harry and less like the healthcare system in the US? It turns out that simplicity is a choice, and having a few tools to help you continually embed it into your process will help boost your superpower #5. No matter what it is that you do, you can Untangle Complexity and find yourself on the road to simplicity in no time.

Tool #1: Edit, Edit, Edit Till You Drop

Anyone can make something complicated, but very few can make it simple. To show you how rare simplicity is at work, consider that 81% of leaders, according to a recent Deloitte study,[31] found that complexity is one of the biggest challenges. That means that most people at work are not trained to declutter complexity. The good news is that by using my system you will be one of the few able to implement simplicity.

The first tool you can use to Untangle Complexity and welcome simplicity is to edit all that you do to its purest form. What do I mean by edit? Editing for simplicity is all about making a decision as to what to keep, what to discard, and sometimes what to change. It's not always about a subtractive choice (like the research study discussed in the previous section), but sometimes just changing things slightly makes simplicity shine.

Edit, Edit, Edit Till You Drop is a system that will give you the ability to edit complexity out, no matter where you are in your career or business. It gives you an awareness of the many sequences in our daily workplace where embedding simplicity in all that we do becomes a choice. That means literally cutting out or changing any unnecessary items that may tempt us to complicate things, which as we've learned is our natural bent. As you get more comfortable with the Edit, Edit, Edit Till You Drop system, a newly attuned alarm will warn you that complexity is unnecessary, allowing you to declutter it.

This process of thinking embeds creativity and innovation in our decision-making because the very system of making the decision in the first place causes us to analyze for complexity and forces us to do the hard work it takes to make something simple. And using this tool in superpower #5 will make you among the few who are able to Untangle Complexity and make it simple for all.

How do we do this? To start, we will look at common touchpoints at work where this tool can be effective. You will likely find a bunch of opportunities to Edit, Edit, Edit Till You Drop and hopefully spur some editing capabilities that you never knew you had, making you one of the few who can simplify instead of the many who complicate.

1. **Email.** Devising a strategy of simplicity in your email communications can be a great place to start to Edit, Edit, Edit Till You Drop. To systemize simplicity in your communications, always start the day by checking the first five emails that you send. Literally open your email program and go to the Sent folder to see what your first five emails looked like. I am certain that you will see paragraph after paragraph written about some complex issue going on at work, with no end in sight for simplicity. Look at the words that you choose to write and start to tune an internal alarm that triggers whenever unnecessary complexity arises, be it a particular topic, your choice of words, a complicated explanation, or unspecific thought. Do you see some patterns emerging? Is it a particular topic or an exchange with an individual team member that is triggering complexity in the email communication? Is it a disposition to complicate something

that you can make simpler with a bit of effort? That internal alarm is a good thing, and noticing patterns where complexity arises will help with this next step. Now open a new email that you would like to respond to. Take all the warning signs from the previously sent emails, and keep them fresh in your head. Begin to write, conscious of the fact that the first five emails you sent earlier may not have been your best. And just keeping that in mind will help you approach this new email with a sense of simplicity. Even if it seems harder at first, it is well worth the effort. That simplicity in communication will get better and better each day that you implement the approach. Remember, every day read the first five emails that you send and continually improve your sensitivity to simplicity in order to communicate better.

2. **Presentations.** Do you create long-winded decks that go on for 82 slides? Do you find yourself rambling on and on during conference calls? If so, this Edit, Edit, Edit Till You Drop presentation tool is for you. Look at every one of your presentation preparations as a challenge. Ask yourself the following question each time you set out to devise a presentation: how can I get my message across in the simplest, most effective way? The important part here is simplicity, whether you are preparing a presentation slide show or a keynote address or a call with the board. When I challenged some of my consulting and keynote clients with this tool, they created a presentation with a few slides, yet managed to jam pack every slide with more information than anyone could ever hope to keep up with. That's not simplicity. Doing that is not getting across the message in the simplest way; it is just limiting the number of slides you choose to show. Real simplicity means changing and editing out anything that is not essential – indeed editing till you drop. The point here is to

challenge yourself to use the fewest words, images, graphics, and charts that will convey your point in the quickest amount of time with the best chance for impact. Yes it's hard. And it forces you to really think about what to keep in, and what to leave out. Ask for help; get feedback on your presentation from people you trust. The section that you think is fool-proof may just be a sticking point that someone else does not understand. All that technical jargon that you used? It may be unnecessary because not everyone is in the weeds like you are. That data that you think your presentation revolves around? Maybe it's not as impactful as you first thought. Finally, go through your presentation material, and ask yourself what the intent of the presentation is. What is it that you want the recipients to feel, understand, or take away? In other words, why are you doing this? Ask yourself this question after you review each slide, and make sure it passes the "why is this important" test. If you cannot answer that question for every slide, then cut it out or change it.

The intent of the presentation first and foremost should always be to get your message across in the simplest most effective way. And understanding what you intend your audience to take away from the presentation is one of the most important tests you can conduct on the efficacy of this particular form of communication. If it doesn't culminate in a very specific action, thought, feeling, or directive for your audience, that is your final warning to change it and Edit, Edit, Edit Till You Drop. None of this is quick, none of this is easy. But if you consistently apply these tools to the design of any presentation, creativity and innovation are likely to be born from the process – and your chances of success will be greatly enhanced.

3. **Organization.** Is your work area a pigsty? Physical work environments have a significant effect on us at the workplace in ways that researchers are just beginning to understand.[32,33] The basic premise of this research is showing that clutter and disorganization at the physical workplace area (workstation, desk, office, bay, etc.) can lead to not only more mistakes,[34] but also a whole host of other maladies like emotional exhaustion, lack of energy at work, and even poor job satisfaction.

    Cleaning up your workplace is no longer about its being unsightly or cluttered, now it is about improving job performance, accuracy at work, and job satisfaction. So what can be done? Regularly tidy up your work area so that you do a little at a time over a long period of time, rather than every once in a while. Hauling over a trash bin and throwing everything out may feel good once a year, but the Edit, Edit, Edit Till You Drop tool encourages this to be a habit, not a once-a-year cleanout. The approach is more of an ongoing maintenance that clears clutter, allowing you to work better in your physical environment. Even if you work remotely, from home, or on the road, having systems that help you keep that clutter in check and using consistent tools (like a note pad and pen) that are typical in your process can boost creativity and innovation. This tool is not about the elimination of clutter altogether. The point is not to sterilize your physical work environment to the point of no return. This is simply a method of regular upkeep of your physical environment to help you recognize opportunities to Edit, Edit, Edit Till You Drop and hopefully spur some creative capabilities by removing complexity. It's about developing a system of editing till you drop so that your ability to simplify otherwise complex matters makes you thrive.

The Edit, Edit, Edit Till You Drop tool can be used for physical clutter or making a better presentation, but it also can be used to simplify communication. It may be hard at first to implement because we are wired for complexity – but ultimately making the choice to Edit, Edit, Edit Till You Drop will show significant dividends on your road to Untangle Complexity.

Tool #2: End the Tyranny of Endless Decisions

What if I were to tell you that there is a magical tool that will allow you to focus on your priorities at work instead of spending your days making endless decisions that seemingly go nowhere? What if there were a purposeful way to make decisions that are directly correlated with your long-term goals? What if instead of becoming overwhelmed by the volume of decisions, you could focus on the ones that matter? Competing priorities at work can often feel so overwhelming that our brains shut down in the fog of complexity – which, in turn, shuts down creative problem solving. Yet focusing on a few key priorities can eliminate that fog and help you to reach and exceed your goals. So how are we doing as a whole managing priorities?

Not so good.

Most people spend too much time at work busy being busy. Being busy is not the same as being productive. It never ceases to amaze me that we associate activity with achievement or productivity – but nothing is further from the truth. Activity for activity's sake is just adding complexity while losing sight of a purposeful end game or goal. It's like planting apple trees and hoping that they produce oranges. It's not going to happen!

Making a quick decision to throw trees in the ground won't get you the right trees. Making another quick decision to dump 20 gallons of water on the roots each day won't get the trees to grow well. And making another quick decision to rip out the apple trees doesn't get us oranges, either. When we spend time being busy for busyness's sake, we produce nothing useful, except perhaps the perception of being busy.

But the perception of being busy fools no one – right? There is no way that someone at work who merely looks busy is taken seriously for being busy? Right? Well, unfortunately no. The perception of being busy is often esteemed at work and thought of as being important.[35] Folks who are busy are seen as "go getters" and "dedicated to the job," yet all this busywork is attuned to driving perception only – nothing more, nothing less. Take the endless meetings we are in, for example. A recent study[36] has shown that somewhere near 70% of our day-to-day meetings keep us from being more productive. They add complexity and busyness at the expense of focusing on priorities and productivity that drive results.

What can we do to End the Tyranny of Endless Decisions that just prove how "busy" we are instead of actually allowing us to accomplish what we set out to do?

Instead of all that busywork for busyness's sake, purposefully choosing to focus on one thing instead of making endless decisions can be incredibly liberating. Making a *purposeful choice* is the secret to unlocking this tool, and Untangling Complexity, and making simple choices that really matter. Doing so is straightforward if we ask ourselves the right questions, regardless of whether we're setting up our own priorities or priorities are determined for us.

Here's how it works: make a list of your business priorities. Limit the list to the top four items you wish to accomplish that quarter. Make the list with pen and paper and update it every three months. As you are making the list, ask yourself the following questions to evaluate each priority:

1. Will this matter to me in five years?
2. Am I concerned about the outcome of this task in the long run?
3. Is this a fleeting stressor or a permanent obstacle?
4. Improvise your own question(s) here.

These questions will help you focus on your goals and determine your list of priorities that will always guide any decision you make to simplify your journey. When guided with a set of plans and a clear, uncomplicated direction, it is far easier to say no to that redundant meeting because you don't need to prove how busy you are to anyone else. The results will speak for themselves.

This is not about making endless decisions that have no ramifications; this is about being purposeful with your decision-making. The outcome of increased creativity and innovation will emerge from the natural selections you make based on your list of priorities, and, finally, these priorities will also allow you to Untangle Complexity and focus on the things that truly matter.

Tool #3: The Silo Killer

Late at night in one Midwestern town, a killer is on the loose, going from silo to silo looking for the next victim. The Silo Killer is not a real person, and it is not looking to harm anyone; in fact, the opposite is true. The Silo Killer is the third tool with the funny name in the quest to Untangle Complexity that will help you once and for all to tear down silos that are keeping things complicated.

Having consulted with some of the biggest and best companies in the world in software, medical, manufacturing, finance, and other industries, I am often asked for creative input to help improve the flow of ideas, processes, and compliance across departments. The problem I almost always encounter is that no one talks to one another. There is no communication between the siloed departments. I have observed teams of the best minds in the country – many with more than one PhD – who have built highly siloed environments where one department doesn't talk to another. It seems that some of the brightest minds are hesitant about sharing information and research, and what ends up happening is that the information stays with them and is not used across the organization, where the knowledge could actually be put to good use.

The problem has two layers. First, the info is not getting shared across silos. This creates lost opportunities for people in other departments. The info has the potential to move the needle in ways that its researchers/owners never could have predicted – even with all those PhDs. Yet, by not sharing it, the opportunity is lost.

The amazing wonder that most people never think about is that people with different backgrounds consume information in different ways. That means that people who aren't researchers may look at the research in ways that the researchers never imagined. That is true for salespeople looking at research and development results, and it's just the same as finance people looking at customer satisfaction surveys. But no one thinks to connect the dots. The common attitude is that sales needs to focus on sales and researchers need to focus on research.

This often results in substantial missed opportunities. For example, the team working on the new biologics has no idea that the marketing people can make a big play in that area because pop culture is attuned to it. Or the new loan program that the bankers came up with is great for new clients, but new clients don't know about it because the info has not been shared with the new client onboarding team.

What ends up happening is that the information gets hoarded, and not shared, and the people who may need the info the most don't get it. People want to protect the integrity of their information and don't believe it's possible to translate their ideas in ways other people can understand. Especially within a company. But without a clear understanding of one another's work, teams have no way to integrate their assignments and tackle their truly big problems. So what can be done? What can we use to help break down silos – be it across an organization or within a department or group? Here are a few things you can use to break down silos, and they all revolve around my favorite number, three:

1. **Write Like a Third Grader.** There are some truly smart people in the world who I am humbled to work with. Some surpass genius level. But when you ask them to explain their software, research, or go-to-market approach, it sounds very, very complicated. They have no way of communicating simply so others can derive the basics of what they are doing because they tend to fall into the complexity bias we learned about earlier in this chapter. One of the things I recommend for these geniuses of industry, and others who may have difficulty with simplifying their ideas, is to Write Like a Third Grader. Write down the idea that they are trying to convey as if they are writing for a third grader to read and consume. It's powerful because it is simple. That jargon that only their department recognizes? Can't use it. A third grader wouldn't understand. That complexity explaining the new regulation? Forget about it. A third grader doesn't even know what regulation means. Write Like a Third Grader is a quick and easy

way to also check if your communication is clear, simple, and easy to understand. It not only works as an exercise that some genius can do, but it is also a good tool to use from time to time for the rest of us when you want to make sure you are Untangling Complexity and offering your thoughts to a wider audience. Write Like a Third Grader is sure to break down silos because of its sheer clarity. Everyone now gets it, and, using simplicity, the communication will help break down even the most rigid silos.

2. **Read Before a Meeting.** In modern business, just about no one reads anything. Having spent an eye-watering amount of time with legal teams over the years, I can imagine how difficult this may be to hear for lawyers who slave over every word. But the truth is, almost no one actually reads anything. Even contracts. I am ashamed to admit that I didn't even read the contact for this book that Wiley sent me. I just signed. So instead of assuming that someone read your Write Like a Third Grader memo before the meeting, read it together. I know that may seem like a colossal waste of time, but reading the passage together in the meeting makes sure that not only has everyone seen the communication, but that they have read it, too. You can read it out loud or carve out time for folks to read it on their own while in the meeting.

   By making this part of the meeting instead of assuming that others are caught up and have read it beforehand, you create cohesion – and yes, simplicity – by simply connecting the dots for everyone.

3. **Write a Maximum of Three-Line Emails for a Week.** Another thing that I recommend is the three-line email. Assume you have written like a third grader, and then made

time for people to read your communication or read it out loud together in a meeting. The last step, which will help break down even the most ensconced silos, is writing three-line emails for a week.

What you do here is take any emails that you send over an average week and cut them all down to the essential message you would like to communicate. Three sentences max. Restrict yourself in that email, text, voicemail, or any other communication with a maximum of three sentences, no matter what you need to convey or respond to. Now, we know that most people don't read anything at work, but distilling your thoughts into just three short sentences enables the message to get across because – even if all we have done is open the email or listen to the voicemail – it's short.

The best part of this Silo Killer is that it's unusual. Most emails are not three sentences – they are either quick yes or no answers or entire paragraphs to read through. But when you send three-line emails for a week, the novelty of such a communication makes it cut through the noise and help be seen.

Write Like a Third Grader is guaranteed to be your own personal Silo Killer each time you encounter it at work. Silos can squeeze any creativity, imagination, or innovation out of any organization. And learning how to deal with silos and untangle their complexity by chipping away at their seemingly unmovable foundation will yield impactful results. The worst thing you can do when encountering silos is nothing – that is how they have gotten to where they are today. By using tool #3 you will now be armed with a way to increase communication.

Conclusion

In this chapter we dove into the fifth superpower and all the ways we can Untangle Complexity to allow for a Solution Mindset to emerge. We saw the amazing miracle of transformation that the Japanese made after WWII, we examined the amazing In-N-Out Burger restaurants that draw folks in from all over the world with their simplicity and dedication to fantastic food, and, finally, we explored complexity bias and found out that we all have it in us to make things more complicated. We wrapped up by learning some tools for Untangling Complexity to focus on simple, easy-to-understand solutions that we can apply no matter what it is that we do. Now we will look at superpower #6, which helps us always Look on the Positive Side of life, no matter what happens to us – or to our careers or businesses.

6

Superpower #6: Look on the Positive Side

What Hiring People with Disabilities Teaches Us About Hidden Treasures

Society should always strengthen its weakest link.

—Gil Winch

November 26, 2001, was a bad day for Gil Winch. At a routine doctor's office visit he had learned he had just a few more months to live. Terminal cancer was the diagnosis. And the doctor delivered the news in a very matter-of-fact way. Clinical. Almost like delivering the weather. Not with empathy or understanding, but cold.

The immediate thought that Gil had was unlike what most of us would think. Most of us would be shocked or cry or scream

105

or feel the overwhelming fear that our lives were soon to be over. Most of us would simply be dazed. Stunned. But not Gil. The first thought that came to his mind upon hearing the news from his doctor was one of defiance. "I'm gonna outlive this guy," Gil thought to himself.

Before that fateful day in November, Gil's life had been going pretty well. He was married to the love of his life, had completed a PhD in psychology (as did his twin brother, Guy), and started a very successful organizational psychology company, working with some of the world's most beloved brands as his clients. He was always keenly interested in the way the mind works and the control it has over body and spirit. And perhaps most importantly, he was always guided by the light of positivity.

To those who know Gil, his next decision was not at all surprising. Upon hearing his diagnosis, he looked at what was in his control instead of what was out of his control. He could control his mind, as he knew from his training. But could he also control his body? He set out to strengthen his body and mind.

He decided that he would start running at the age of 40, having never run so much as to catch a cab before. He would enter a marathon and train his body for the grueling endurance race. He also started to strengthen his mind by looking at a new mission to serve others in his day-to-day at work – one that was set up to help as many people as possible. He had no idea what that would be, but he was open to finding out. He then shut down his thriving practice, closing the consulting company forever. It was not meeting his new mission to serve others in a way that would be beneficial to the greatest number of people possible. Gil's new focus was to be on body and mind. Nothing more, nothing less.

At a party one night shortly thereafter, he met a friend who was disabled. This friend had been in a wheelchair his whole life and complained about being habitually unemployed his entire career. That one comment would haunt Gil as he went home that night. He knew one thing for sure: The war for talent – for fantastic people to hire – had become the new normal for so many organizations who struggled finding qualified and skilled candidates. He knew that from his own experience. An idea emerged. He was fixated on it. How can it be that simply because someone is disabled, they cannot get hired, find work, and are otherwise excluded from the job market? Why is it that people with disabilities are overlooked by hiring managers and HR professionals because of their disability? What Gil saw that night was a wonderful friend, capable in every single way, someone deserving of the same opportunities in the workforce as someone who is not disabled. Someone deserving of the dignity of work.

And that's when it hit him like a ton of bricks. Could this be his new calling? Could he connect the corporate need to find and hire talent with people with disabilities – an untapped gold mine of talent in the workforce? The excitement of that potential discovery led Gil to research disability and the unemployment of people with disabilities, and what he found was staggering:

- People with disabilities show chronically low rates of employment,[1] and are three times more likely[2] to be unemployed[3] than people without disabilities.

- When they do finally attain employment, people with disabilities earn drastically lower wages than people without disabilities[4] – often for the same roles.

- Often, employers deliberately don't hire people with disabilities simply because of various stigmas around disabilities,[5] and if they do they hire only one or two candidates before giving up.

Gil started to ask himself some profound questions, one of which was: how this could be? In a population full of folks like

Gil's friend, who was more than competent, willing, and able to work, why weren't they getting hired? Also, why do employers view people with disabilities in a negative light, full of stigmas and shameful pessimism, and with downright unfriendliness? This one conversation he had at a party, and his research, led him to find new drive and purpose in life.

By looking for the positive, Gil began to see a side of life that others miss. A hidden untapped treasure: people with disabilities joining the workforce.

He started a company called Call Yachol, or CY for short, and he set out to hire people with disabilities to show companies that they could become great employees – if they were managed correctly! Here was this great reservoir of untapped talent that could solve many staffing difficulties for companies of all sizes! Easy peasy, right?

Well, no.

Gil hit roadblock after roadblock, including some of the very systems designed to help people with disabilities. First, he hit a dreadful roadblock when interviewing people with disabilities, asking them a very simple question: Why are you unemployed? Most people that he talked to wanted to work so that they could contribute to society and improve their lot. They happened to be blind, deaf, paralyzed, or had a myriad of other disabilities but were otherwise capable of doing the job they applied for. Yet time and time again, many weren't even invited for an interview, and those who were hired were often promptly fired.

Beyond that, many chronically unemployed people with disabilities face numerous emotional difficulties acquired by years of social isolation and the financial struggles that minimal government financial support brings, regardless of what their "official disability" (blind, deaf, etc.) actually is. Employers didn't have the necessary tools to help people with disabilities to break free from these shackles, and after a failed attempt or two, they stopped trying to hire people with disabilities altogether. Indeed, Gil found that a high proportion of people with disabilities are on anti-depressants[6] and other meds to help them deal with the social isolation that accompanies chronic unemployment.

But here is where it gets even trickier. Government assistance programs designed to help people with disabilities unfortunately often make things worse. The government tries to help by offering financial-assistance benefit programs that pay a disabled person *not* to work. This is often an insufficient sum, based on the assumption that people with disabilities cannot get jobs because they are blind, deaf, or have some other disability. And even if they can work, government reasoning goes on to state that people with disabilities won't likely earn more than the government's paltry assistance[7] in the first place.

There is a fundamental problem with the government's reasoning however. It unfortunately results in helping people barely survive instead of thrive. Many people with disabilities are some of the greatest assets society can possibly have and are wealthy as a result, and their work is not only important but also very profitable. Gil found that to be the case, too, and therefore spent many years battling government institutions that seemed to be entrenched in a bureaucracy that made it even more difficult for people with disabilities to successfully join the job market and even more daunting for potential employers to hire them.

Given these challenges Gil could have thrown in the towel at anytime and focused instead on working to improve his health in light of his terminal cancer diagnosis. But instead of quitting, these roadblocks energized him! He found ways to view the situation in a positive way instead of focusing on the negative. Proving to the world that people with disabilities can successfully join the job market, demonstrate strong productivity, and earn competitive wages could alleviate so much unnecessary suffering. The managerial model Gil had developed and perfected at CY had the potential to provide employers with the tools they would need to successfully employ people with disabilities. It could also provide a real hope for a better future to the majority of the one billion people with disabilities in the world who were out of a job and were struggling for their financial survival.

So he got to work. He built an outsourced call center focused on providing customer service with, to date, 250 employees. He devised a whole new managerial model, new HR positions and practices, and new screening and onboarding techniques. His work on behalf of, and with, people with disabilities received international recognition, including sharing a stage with President Bill Clinton, a TED Talk, op-eds, citations in major publications, and numerous awards. He has had people reach out and visit the call center from over 80 counties to learn what the "secret sauce" is and how they can apply it to their own businesses and national programs.

His business today is as profitable as any other similarly sized call center – with a workforce comprised of 80% people with disabilities (including managers and staff, most of whom had never worked before), and 20% people previously incarcerated and ethnic minorities. CY often exceeds both revenue and profitability goals each year while maintaining a culture characterized by human warmth and caring and happy employees.

How did Gil manage to do all this? He started by focusing on the positive instead of the negative. When most employers saw someone disabled, they made that disability a negative. A missing limb, a wheelchair, a cognitive disability, deafness, or blindness became a negative. Gil instead focused on the entire package of the person – looking at the person as a whole instead of stigmatizing them for their disability. And in that, he found an untapped wealth of new workplace hires.

I know for sure that, countless times, I have fallen into the trap of not hiring on the positive but instead getting fixated on the negative. Looking at that weakness in the resume – looking at that gap in industry employment or a less-than-stellar interview led to my passing over an otherwise qualified candidate to hire. But I wonder how many fantastic people I have missed out on because I was too busy focusing on the negative instead of looking at the positive. It's a mindset shift that needs to be made from negative to positive, one that can bring substantial benefit to you and your organization.

And if that wasn't enough, Gil is now starting a new company that seeks to employ people with cognitive disabilities in much the same way that CY has worked for people with physical, sensory, and emotional disabilities.

Gil chose to look at the positivity that came along with the whole person. And in it he found some of the most dedicated workforce he has ever had the pleasure to work alongside. He calls them the "underdogs." And these underdogs now have grown to include veterans, who often have a tough time getting hired in civilian roles, and convicted felons, who work for CY while still doing prison time. Likewise, we make the choice every day to choose how we view others. For Gil and his team, it's all about looking for the hidden potential that each person has.

Cross-Pollination

Sometimes the next big idea is hidden right under your nose. Just like Gil has found hidden treasures in people with disabilities who are amazing hires in a world that is constantly hungry for a new talent pool, I also actively hunt for the next big thing. But I don't do it within my industry. I do it within other industries.

Each year, I go to tradeshows, events, and conferences, not to keynote the event or sign books, but instead to see what other people are doing in far-flung industries that are radically different from the consulting, publishing, or events and conference industries that I actively work in. I go in with a sense of positivity – actively looking to be inspired. I learned to go to other industry trade shows by accident because I do a fair amount of consulting in industries like aviation, financial services, and manufacturing, which sort of forced me to be exposed to a wider variety of industries outside my own. I didn't initially set out to do it, but what I found was game changing and is now part of my regular yearly schedule.

One of the most amazing things that I found by being exposed to industries outside my own was that they inspire new ideas in my own consulting and keynote work. But we have to go into the experience with a positivity mindset away from skepticism. It's amazing what kind of insight you can derive when looking at the positive. You can spend some time outside of your industry, immersed in another industry that has perhaps already solved many of the problems that you are facing, yet these solutions would be fresh and new in your industry. When we look outside our current environment for inspiration, we may come across ideas so powerful and so convincing that they may be novel in our industry, despite being commonplace in another industry. I call this approach *cross-pollination*.

Here are some inspiring examples of cross-pollination that I hope spur you to begin the practice in your own industry:

1. **Loyalty Programs.** Loyalty programs have been around for a while; one author traced loyalty programs back to the 18th century in the stamp trading business.[8] Loyalty program popularity in modern times has caught on especially in aviation

with the airline industry. The early 1980s saw airlines trying to figure out a way to differentiate their airline from competitors, so they came up with loyalty programs redeemable as miles or points.[9] The basic premise is the same today as it was back then: the more you spend with one airline, the more benefits you get with that particular brand. It may be a complimentary upgrade. It may be a free meal or a better boarding time. In each case, the basic arrangement is to allow for a more predictable revenue stream from a set customer base while incentivizing that customer behavior to continually pick the same airline, even if there are other, cheaper fares available. It is quite brilliant. Why would you try to save a bit of money by flying another airline when just a few more points would get you that upgrade?

Soon after, the hotel industry cross-pollinated the airline idea into the hotel industry, albeit with different incentives. Instead of offering an upgraded seat or a better boarding time, hotels like Marriott offered points that add up to free stays and upgraded views. Marriott had cross-pollinated an idea from airline loyalty programs and offered it to their customers with similar success. Why stay at a cheaper hotel when just a few more points would get you that better hotel view or a free night to use at your leisure?

This cross-pollination from aviation to the hotel business is how loyalty programs really got going since the early 1980s, and today they are found everywhere from supermarkets to restaurants. And it proved that a good idea within one industry just well may be a good idea in another industry.

2. **Video Games.** The video game industry has been around for quite some time, but gained momentum in the late 1970s

with the Atari 2600, which was the most successful system of its generation, selling more than 30 million units.[10] What the Atari 2600 did so well was that it allowed multiple game cartridges to be played on the same system, so that users only had to buy one system and one controller to be able to play a collection of games.

Then, the games themselves were engaging and fun – and perhaps most importantly – they kept score. Every time you played games like Space Invaders, Pac Man, or the first video game ever designed by a woman, River Raid,[11] you would get points. And that would add up to some impressive bragging rights for you and your friends, tapping into that innate human desire for personal achievement and advancement among peers.

Then, the educational industry cross-pollinated from the video game industry, bringing points into learning material. With the popularity of gaming simply for fun or bragging rights, why not make the goal the gamification of educational material instead, tapping into those same human desires to achieve and advance, but this time for learning. The educational industry cross-pollinated to make learning a video game, where the goal was not to get high points, but to learn a certain topic like math or geography and get rewarded for it by earning an achievement badge or points.

Today, the results are incredible. It was found that students who use gamification-based learning cross-pollinated from that Atari 2600 all those years ago saw improved student performance of 89.4% compared to lecture-based learning with overall student performance improvements of 34.7%[12] when used as part of the educational curriculum. What a great way to use one industry's innovation and cross-pollinate it to another.

3. **Space-Age Materials.** The space program is continually looking to achieve a reduction in weight while maintaining a rigid structure to their spacecraft, which has to yield to incredible forces of acceleration in the hostile environment of our atmosphere and space. And the reason is simple: costs. It costs quite a bit of money to put a rocket into orbit and to carry its payload or astronauts up in space, and any reduction in weight means an increase in payload size and less fuel consumed, a winning combination to lower costs.

During the early 1960s, a material was used in the aerospace industry called carbon fiber, which itself was cross-pollinated from the light bulb industry 70 years before in the late 19th century,[13] to make components of a rocket that were to be structurally sound yet weigh less.

This use of carbon fiber was then used in the space shuttle program for the nose cap and the leading edges of the wings,[14] and shortly thereafter spread to all sorts of parts and structures within other spacecraft to further reduce weight and reenforce structural integrity.

Then the automotive industry cross-pollinated the carbon fiber from spacecraft material to automobile material to improve crash protection and aerodynamic efficiencies. Some automotive manufacturers even left the carbon fiber as a decoration item exposed within their cars so that people could see it, which looks like a hologram of woven metallic threads. Ultimately, carbon fiber would enhance structural integrity and reduce weight just like it did for the aerospace industry. Taking one industry's big idea just may lead to a big idea in your industry, as the implementation of carbon fiber has done in many different industries.

Drawing insights from unrelated fields to drive cross-pollination can lead to some incredible benefits in your industry. Being exposed to what other industries are doing and seeing them firsthand at trade shows, events, and conferences can be a life-changing experience. So how do we cross-pollinate using positivity as our driver? How can we be more like Gil Winch in finding hidden treasure that no one has paid attention to before?

Tool #1: Use Better Words

Our quest for positivity to enhance our creative and innovative ideas starts with the very words that we choose to use. Every time we speak or write, we are selecting a series of words to convey our thoughts. The way we appear to others as we communicate is largely a product of the words that we choose.

When was the last time you took some time out to think carefully about your words? Far too often we are careless with our word selection. We hope that people will get what we are trying to say without focusing on the intent and impact of the words that we choose. I began to notice this early in my consulting work with different teams, across companies of all sizes. I noticed something strange going on with my clients and their communication.

Communication just wasn't working, and communication breakdowns were occurring in almost every written and verbal interaction.

I was seeing entire projects lost to semantics and unclear word selection. And people using words in ways that invited conflict instead of resolution or creativity. I saw otherwise-successful people locked in head-to-head arguments simply on a missed interpretation of a word in an email or contract or even a voicemail communication. Circular logic about trying to determine whether what was said was what was actually meant wasted countless hours.

What do all of these things have in common? I noticed it was the choice of words people would use in business, at the office, in emails, texts, on Zoom calls – and especially – how and why these words were being selected that caused the communication breakdown. For example, one client I had seemed to have an all too familiar culture of negativity in their communication. In a Slack message during meetings, I noticed that people would write this meeting is "unproductive" and "awful." It was the way that things were communicated at that company, and it was part of the everyday culture. Similarly, I noticed this client didn't celebrate their wins and use positive language in describing them. Instead of saying "nice work" when it was going well, it was "well at least we didn't get fired" and instead of "that went great and job well done" it was "we live to fight another day."

I noticed right then with that particular client that the English language is incredibly biased in favoring negative words over positive words. How can that be? For the past 1,500 years that the English language has been spoken, its users were literally fighting for basic existence in lawless times rife with plague, wars, and famine, so it's no surprise that there are more ways to describe something negatively than positively in English! But then I felt I had to dig a bit deeper.

So deeper I dug and found that there is roughly a six-to-one[15,16] ratio of negative words for positive words in English! It's impossible to count every word in every language, but the overall imbalance of word selection in English remains true. Isn't that amazing?! So for every word that is positive, let's say, "Fantastic," there are six times more negative words like "Horrible," "Bad," "Terrible," "Awful," "Gross," and "Nasty." Six times more negative words than positive!

Why in the world is this the case? The best explanation I found is that, from an evolutionary perspective, communities that developed more negative words than positive ones were more likely to survive and thrive. There was a need for negativity in language because it was used as a warning to not eat this "nasty" red berry or drink that "disgusting" water and so on – literally a system developed to keep humans alive. The negative-to-positive word ratio had a purpose back then.

But what about today? We are no longer driven solely by survival – especially at work. Negative words today carry more harm than positive words. In a recent study, participants placed in an MRI machine and exposed to pain-related or negative words reported experiencing more intense pain than those exposed to neutral or positive words![17] So how does negativity over positivity in language effect the modern workforce? Well, it turns out quite a bit.[18] Because the hardwired linguistic negativity in our language, held over from our ancestors, isn't needed today for survival, it destroys cohesive and clear communications. And that is what I saw with my consulting clients.

So what can we do? Well, the good news is a lot! The awareness of our language and choosing positivity can make us more creative[19] and innovative at work so we communicate more clearly.[20] This leads to a whole host of other positive benefits, including making us easier to work with, more competitive[21] in the marketplace, better understood, better liked, and more empathetic.[22] Here are a few principles and examples of how we can take these findings on the importance of using positive language at work and apply them in our day-to-day communication.

Prioritize Clarity and Creativity Over Efficiency

In our day-to-day rush to get more and more done across all channels of communication (as we are more connected today than ever) we tend to rush into things at work. Nonstop. Go. Go. Go. If we instead pause for only a few seconds before we send that text or voicemail or email, we can be far better prepared to use the language of positivity. We need to be willing to sacrifice efficiency for clarity and creativity.

It's okay to slow down and get it right. It's okay to take the time we need to be clear and to choose positive words out of all the options in our lexicon.

There is nothing that says you need to hit send the moment after writing an email! This is not a race for the swift, it's a race for those who best endure. Take a minute. Pause. Take an hour, or even a few days. Take a deep and satisfying breath. Make sure that communication says exactly what you want it to say. Have someone else read it to make sure. Sometimes when the work world moves at breakneck speeds, the folks who are able to pause the blur and focus on what they want to say select their language carefully and with intention.

Measure Yourself

Every day for a week, examine the last 20 emails you sent at work. Count the negative versus positive words you used. See if, over the span of a week, you can gradually manage to use more positive than negative words, or if you at least improve over the previous check. Most people inadvertently choose negative words to describe things, so check in with yourself and listen to how you are using words.

A recent study showed a direct correlation between having negative thoughts and the chance of those negative thoughts actually manifesting.[23] It seems that you are what you think. It's up to each one of us to make sure that we have maximum positivity injected into our thoughts and words if we ever hope to communicate clearly.

Being positive with our language is a choice – and when we Use Better Words, our interactions at work and beyond become more pleasurable, more clear, more impactful, better understood, and better for our overall health. So just by using this one simple tool, you can take back your language and make communication positive and full of opportunity for creativity and innovation—not just today, but for the rest of your life.

Tool #2: Newton's Third Law

The best bosses I have ever had in my career have been the bad ones. The ones that are late and demand that you come in on time. The ones that swindle and then check to make sure no one else is doing it. The ones that skim a few bucks off the till, the ones that yell. And in each case, I could have looked at it as a hardship, or a disadvantage, but I didn't. I chose to look at it in a positive way using tool #2, which I will share with you here, and which I am certain will transform the way you look at disadvantage and turn it into an advantage.

To help with that, I borrowed from Isaac Newton's Third Law, which states simply that for every action, there is an equal and opposite reaction. When applied to our daily challenges at work, this is all about changing your perspective on every action that you deem offensive, bothersome, or just downright drudging – and channeling that action instead into an equal and opposite reaction.

It is sometimes so very hard to be positive at work. Believe me, I get it. There are times when choosing positivity can be such a challenge and can test your very resolve. And yet, at these exact times, it is especially important to choose to look at whatever happens in a positive way as much as humanly possible, given the situation.

I have been working since I was nine years old. And readers of my other books know that I started going door to door washing cars and I worked at Subway Restaurants as a sandwich artist long before I had my own company. And in each case, I have had my fair share of horrible bosses, people who did far more wrong than they did right. Some of them did it all wrong with no room for right because they were that far gone.

But here is the really cool part of tool #2, Newton's Third Law, applied to my superpower of positivity: you get to choose how you view these horrible bosses. So instead of thinking, "my boss is overly demanding or terrible," think of all the positive things that can come out of that situation.

In no way am I diminishing the fact that your boss is difficult, but I am asking you to shift your mindset. Yes, for sure, your boss is a jerk, but what can you learn *not* to do from him? Sometimes the greatest value you can learn from others is not what *to* do, but what *not* to do. So if your boss is overly demanding and a jerk, then begin to pay attention to the opposite of what they are doing. That mindset can be an amazing learning experience so that you know what works and what doesn't. Take a look at the list below for common negative examples of reactions that can turn wonderfully positive with Newton's Third Law, as used in my Solution Mindset:

1. **"I just lost my job"** is not the positive way to look at the situation, given my positivity superpower. Instead, think, "What can I do with all this time, and what is it that I really want to do?" Is it starting that small business? Is it going to work for a different company that you have always admired? Is it taking your current strengths into a new career direction? It's about taking a perceived negative and making it into a positive. I have had my fair share of lost jobs for whatever reason, but in each case, it always led to something better.

2. **"My customers are so demanding"** is not the positive way to look at the situation, given my positivity superpower. Instead, think how great it is that your customers actually want something from you! That they push you to do better

and excel. There are most likely a lot of other places your customers can go to consume your product or service, and here you are thinking about the negative instead of the positive. What kinds of solutions will open up once you think about how great it is indeed that your customers are so demanding! What can you do with that? Would you reinvent a new customer approach? Would you create a virtual drop box for customer concerns? Would you find a way to market your business that shows you're delivering higher quality than your competitors? In each case, looking at what we may see as generally a negative and turning that into a positive with Newton's Third Law gives us opportunities that we never had before we shifted our mindset.

3. **"People keep writing bad reviews"** is not the positive way to look at the situation, given my positivity superpower. Instead, view that as a customer who is craving your interaction and attention who can give valuable feedback. They just want their voice to be heard – so what can you do to listen? You may come up with numerous ideas of how to listen, depending on what industry you happen to be in, but that feedback in the first place is invaluable. If someone took the time to leave a written review, chances are that they actually want to interact with you.

I have been prompted countless times to review everything from credit cards to restaurants to vendors. But I seldom leave written reviews because I just review the interaction directly, in person, because I am that kind of guy. I'd rather just tell someone face to face what I think. But some people are afraid of confrontation and do not want to ask for a manager or tell someone of their difficulty with their product or service, for whatever reason. That doesn't dilute the feedback, and you can still use the so-called bad reviews as a positive opportunity to accept criticism and interact with customers to learn and grow. Any interaction is better than no interaction. Just be sure to keep Tool #1 in mind and Use Better Words. The point is to react to the reviews with positive energy, not defensively.

When we decide to shift our mentality from something negative to embracing the positive, we see many solutions emerge that we may never have seen before. Doing so opens so many creative possibilities to deal with the inevitable bumps in the road. While everyone sees the bumps and the hardships, you instead see the bumps in the road as opportunities to use Newton's Third Law to be positive.

Tool #3: Add a Dose of Humanity

We have forgotten how to treat each other in our day-to-day lives. We seem to value efficiency over relationships; we revere speed over all else. And we have ended up losing our very humanity at work. In the constant huff and haste of modern business, we have forgotten the most important part of being human – the need to connect with each other.

Several studies have been conducted on the overall happiness of human beings all over the world. Just about each study that ranks what makes people the happiest finds that human connection is the one thing – above all else – that consistently makes people happiest. The longest study ever conducted on happiness is the Harvard Study of Adult Development,[24] which started in 1938 and continues to this day. It has found, among other things, that our ability as a species to work together with others is what gives us joy. In other words, it's our connection to each other that gives us the most happiness year after year. So why are we sacrificing some of the most important interactions of our lives on the altar of efficiency? Why are we giving up what makes us happy and fast-forwarding it for speed or data or more, more, more?

We need to get better at adding a dose of humanity in all we do. At the core, this humanity is positive interaction with not only the people we work with but also the world we live in. We are constantly focused on efficiency and analytics and the data on our spreadsheet. But there are immense creative benefits to focusing on the human side of work and living in better balance.

Here are some tools that will help you rediscover a dose of humanity that you can add to your every day, a small slice of how to increase humanity in your interactions:

1. **Be Present.** Make an effort to see prospects, coworkers, or even friends in person. Be present in meetings and on calls. Talk less and listen more. The most effective way to Add a Dose of Humanity to everything that we do is to actually be there, to pick up the phone, to interact on a human level, not always through technology.

   Back to the chapter opening: at his company CY, Gil has instituted a role called the Lioness, which is basically a person whose job it is to help employees with a huge array of life problems that aren't connected to work but impinge on the employee's ability to succeed at work. Issues like foreclosures on their bank accounts, inability to pay a dentist, or lack of a place to sleep for a few nights. The Lioness operates with no budget and relies on kind professionals who volunteer their time to aid those less fortunate than themselves. She is called the Lioness because her job is to protect the cubs – all employees at all levels. It's not only good for the people who work at CY, but it's also good for the bottom line.

   What can you do at work to be more present? Is it perhaps that intern that needs some more attention or coaching in order to do well? Is it making time to talk less in meetings and listen more to realize how others are contributing? No matter what it is, being present and taking time to be in the moment will Add a Dose of Humanity to everything you do at work and beyond.

2. **Address the Human Being in Your Communication.** When you send or receive an email or text, refer to the person in some way, shape, or form before you refer to the task or work subject at hand. Add humanity to your communication. It takes just seconds. Try to inject a personal reference, if possible, or anything that adds humanity like: "How was your kid's first day at kindergarten?" or " I hope all is well and things are going good" is better than "Call Ella first thing in the morning about the proposal" or "Get me the contract; I want to see where it says *that*" with your auto signature. It's more positive to find some common ground – a thread of connection – and address a person as a human being. That increases the likelihood of finding common ground that may just be the next catalyst for innovation and creativity.

3. **Don't Treat People as Transactions.** Lots of folks spend their time at work trying to get something out of the relationships that they have with others. People do that in their lives away from work too. I regularly get asked to read a manuscript or introduce someone to my book agent or to help them get a keynote booked. Although I want to help as much as I can, being treated like a transaction is not a good way to treat anyone, for various reasons.

For instance, some folks may want a promotion and are trying to brownnose their boss. Some may want that new customer to sign up so they try to get the most they can out of the person. Some have other reasons for treating a relationship as a transaction, but when we do this, we lose our humanity and we tend to treat people as objects, rather than people. And people can tell that they are being treated as an object, no matter how cunning, slick, or smooth you think you are being. If we begin to treat each other as human beings with the dignity that we all deserve, it increases the chances of creativity and communication being understood and it makes the world a little bit of a better place to live in.

By filtering your communications through a human lens, you may uncover ways that people who you work with can help you with a problem or help you see your next challenge from a new point of view. This does not happen when we treat people as objects and relationships as transactions. This happens when we treat people with dignity and respect. Positive, human-centered conversations have a way of traveling to surprising places and opening minds to new ideas that would never have come from a quick, transactional interaction.

Conclusion

In this chapter we looked at the sixth superpower and all the ways we can look at the positive side of life. We looked at the incredible and inspirational story of Gil Winch and his company CY making waves in the hiring, retention, and training of people with disabilities. We looked at how cross-pollination and being exposed to industries outside our own can be the next big thing, and finally we looked at how important our selection of language is and how to actively be more positive in all that we do. It's been well over 20 years since Gil was diagnosed with terminal cancer, so it seems that adopting a positive attitude in life is also greatly beneficial to our health. Now we will look at superpower #7 and how routine is one of the best facilitators for creativity and innovation in all that we do, driving a Solution Mindset for our careers and businesses.

7

Superpower #7: Embrace the Routine

What Civil War Reenactments Teach Us About Thinking Inside the Box

History is who we are and why we are the way we are.
—David McCullough

E very year thousands of people descend on the tiny town of Olustee, Florida, in early February. They are not only there to commemorate the Battle of Olustee, which occurred during the Civil War in 1864, but also to recreate it.[1]

The Battle of Olustee was the largest Civil War battle fought in Florida. In 1864, the Union had landed troops in Jacksonville, Florida, roughly 40 miles due east of Olustee, with the goal of disrupting Confederate food supplies that ran up the East Coast with beef, pork, salt, and other food goods. Meeting little resistance initially, the Union General, Truman Seymour, put his 5,500 men on a march toward Tallahassee, seeking to further disrupt shipments of food to Confederate troops, assuming that he would meet limited resistance on the road.

He was wrong.

Resistance arrived in Olustee, led by Confederate General Alfred H. Colquitt and his 5,000 troops. And what emerged was a battle with one of the highest casualties during the Civil War, the second bloodiest battle of the War for the Union, with 265 casualties per 1,000 troops:

- Union casualties were 203 killed, 1,152 wounded, and 506 missing, a total of 1,861 men – about 34% of Union General Truman Seymour's force.[2]

- Confederate losses were 93 killed, 848 wounded, and 8 missing, a total of 949 in all – a fair percentage of Confederate General Alfred H. Colquitt's force, about 19%.[3]

Soldiers on both sides of the Battle of Olustee were veterans of some of the greatest battles in the Civil War, yet many of them remarked in letters and diaries that they had never undergone such terrible fighting.[4] The battle was all but over in four hours. The Union retreated back to Jacksonville while the Confederates retained control of Florida's interior for the rest of the war, which ended a little more than a year later, in April 1865, when Robert E. Lee surrendered to Ulysses S. Grant at Appomattox.

So what draws thousands of people every year to a tiny patch of pine forest to recreate the Battle of Olustee? The battle was an especially important one. First, over 10,000 cavalry, infantry, and artillery troops were involved on both sides. Second, three United States Colored Troops regiments also took part in the battle, including the now-famous 54th Massachusetts Infantry Regiment. One of the first Black units formed during the Civil War, it was originally commanded by Col. Robert Gould Shaw and made famous by the 1989 film *Glory*.[5] And finally, thorough and complete journals and letters written at the time make the Battle of Olustee one of the best documented battles of the Civil War.

And that last point about the documentation of the battle being well preserved is of great interest to the reenactors because the level of detail in their reenactments has to be as close to real as possible based on the historical record. It's the entire point of the reenactment. The reenactors go to great lengths to be accurate and authentic as they Embrace the Routine year after year. Authenticity is everything.

For example, if the troops slept outside without tents during the battle, the modern reenactors do the same – dressed in the same period outfits nonetheless[6]! Wear eyeglasses? Those have to be period correct as well.[7] There is even a protocol and etiquette on how people should "die" during the reenactments. "No one wants to drive hours on end to go to an event and then march out onto the field, fire several rounds and then take a hit and lay on the field for the rest of the battle," said Michael Cheaves, who reenacts with the 1st Tennessee Cavalry in Jefferson City. "It kind of defeats the purpose."[8] So there are provisions set ahead of time for how many people die and how and when they should fall to match the real battle as accurately as possible.

There are also "stitch counters"[9] in the reenactment community, and their job is to be as historically accurate in assessing the uniforms, buttons, and even fabric and shoes of the outfits worn during the reenactment to ensure historical accuracy. The weapons of the time, including correct rifles and cannons, are tirelessly checked for accuracy, given the particular region and regiment issued,[10] and even the horses of the cavalry are period correct. The ultimate goal is not so much a reenactment, as participating in a living history.[11]

A living history tries to get a reenactment as close to authentic as humanly possible. If the 5th Texas Infantry Regiment got new shell jackets for the summer, so did the reenactors. If soldiers marched northwest at dawn, so should the players who reenact the scene. If they ate a meal of hardtack[12] (flour, salt, and water known to keep for years) cooked with bacon and topped with dried apples, that's what reenactors eat. At Olustee and other reenacted Civil War battles, the goal is to play out the scene as closely as possible to the original battle, not just the actual fight, but the moments before and after. Year after year. Time and time again. Olustee has seen 48 consecutive years[13] of Civil War battle reenactment, and each year participants Embrace the Routine to keep the truth alive.

Civil War reenactors, on the surface, may seem like a strange bunch. They spend time driving from historical battlefield to historical battlefield, and on the internet in different chat groups and webpages that have the latest information on battle reenactments. They spend weekends reenacting and trying to create a living history of events that are now over 150 years old. Why in the world would they do this – and indeed are they a strange bunch?

In doing the research for this book, I have found the answer to that question to be an emphatic *no*. And the reasons reenactors participate in these massive reenactments across the country are as varied as the individuals who participate. Some reenactors feel that they are honoring history by committing to portray soldiers accurately and acknowledge their sacrifices. Others have a personal connection, having family history on both sides of the Civil War. Some like the experience of getting dressed up and being someone else for the weekend, others enjoy the reenactor community, which leaves politics at the door and embraces one another warmly.[14] Yet one thing that is a commonality across the Civil War reenactment community is the power of education. Going beyond the textbooks and into the real world brings home an educational value that cannot be measured in anything but experience. Hearing heavy hooves pound the dirt as mounted soldiers cross a ridge, and seeing the Confederate flag wave are stark reminders of a country once divided and now whole. And this is the type of preservation of history – a commemoration – you can't get any other way but by embracing routine year after year.

Commemoration, Corruption, and Creativity

Commemoration is a facet of human ingenuity that earmarks special occurrences that are not ordinary, everyday experiences. It is all about retaining the memory or committing to memory the events, developments, and people from the past in its entirety: the good, the bad, and the ugly.

Take for instance a wedding anniversary or a birthday. It's important to commemorate, and in this case celebrate, the event every year as a routine because that day is rich with meaning. Your birthday is the day you were put on this earth, and a wedding anniversary commemorates the date you and your spouse committed to each other, hopefully for the rest of your lives. That's why we take photos, save guestbooks, and spend a day celebrating important events.

Similarly, when we earmark events like the Battle of Olustee or other important cultural or historical movements, we assign a meaning to those events that we deem important in the collective fabric of our lives. The integrity of that commemoration is paramount. It has to be remembered as it was, and any deviation from the truth corrupts both the commemoration and history itself. The reenactors of the Battle of Olustee keep history alive by restaging the 150-year-old conflict each year, wearing period attire and following historically accurate troop movements. Their efforts stave off the corruption of truth for one more year at a time, preserving memory in a world rife with distortion.

At any given time, anywhere in the world, corruption is indeed rampant. It can take many forms; it can be political corruption or fiscal corruption, historical corruption or a myriad other types of corruption. And in each and every case, the truth is violated for the personal gain of just a few.

Corruption is one of the most prevalent global problems affecting business today.[15] Its widespread effects can be felt in any country on earth, and according to the Transparency International 2023 Corruption Perceptions Index, the United States ranks #24 on the list of most corrupt countries (surprisingly, Denmark, Finland, and New Zealand rank 1, 2, and 3, respectively).

Even more, our routines and commemorations are under threat from a powerful new foe: artificial intelligence (AI). AI perverts history with an array of tools that are especially adept at introducing a fog of confusion. AI's corruption of history and the people who program its data have caused significant issues in recent years. Here are just two of many significant issues with the technology:

1. **Corruption of Images.** AI programs have created fake images of historical events that are so lifelike and real – period

correct – that they are confusing at best and absolutely fake at worst, clouding the actual historical photos from the time.[16] Some of the most dangerous photos are "deep fake" AI photos, which pretty much means a fake so realistic and deep in its details that it fools us – such as fake photos of President John F. Kennedy's assassination,[17] bogus photos of fake disease outbreaks like the Russian Blue Plague,[18] and phony images of people like the pope posing for Balenciaga.[19]

2. **AI Hallucinations.** AI is prone to just making things up – out of the blue. Software developers call this a "hallucination," and it's as if the AI is grabbing at facts and figures that make no sense. It's a hallucination of facts. When viewed in historical context, this hallucination ends up corrupting historical and even contemporary facts, leading to pure fabrication and made up historical connections that have no basis in reality yet seem convincing to people who have no idea of its authenticity.[20] AI often has issues with basic questions that humans can see as being ridiculous like "What's the world record for crossing the English Channel entirely on foot?" AI replies are gibberish like: "The world record for crossing the English Channel entirely on foot is held by Christof Wandratsch of Germany, who completed the crossing in 14 hours and 51 minutes on August 14, 2020."[21] Christof is a swimmer by the way, and the AI has hallucinated an historical answer that sounds plausible but is in fact nonsense.

You may say that there is nothing new under the sun with AI – and that people have been trying to fabricate and readjust and corrupt historical facts to support their personal gain for a very long time. And you would be right. But the prevalence of tools that can easily create these types of hallucinations and photographs is widespread. Now with social media, the threat becomes multifold. Anyone with any opinion on anything can become popular simply because they have some followers who believe them.[22] The accessibility of these tools makes spreading misinformation as easy as typing a prompt into a website. This raises a critical question: who can distinguish the real from the fake? Can we separate authentic historical records – such as the Battle of Olustee or the Civil War itself – from fabricated versions that never happened? And what is truly at stake if we lose our history? David McCullough, one of the finest historians of our time and a two-time winner of both the Pulitzer Prize and the National Book Award, as well as recipient of the Presidential Medal of Freedom, often reminded us: "The best way to know where the country is going is to know where we've been."

Take this quick pop quiz about US history:

- Do you know when the US Constitution was ratified?
- Can you name three states that were part of the original 13 colonies?
- Why did the colonists fight the British[23]?

If you struggled with these questions, don't feel bad. Apparently, so do a lot of people. Here are the answers, along with some sobering statistics:

- Only 13% of those surveyed know when the US Constitution was ratified.[24] (It was June 1, 1788, when New Hampshire became the ninth of 13 states.[25])
- 72% of respondents either incorrectly identified or were unsure of which states were part of the 13 original states.[26] (The original 13 colonies were New Jersey, Maryland, Virginia, Massachusetts, Rhode Island, Connecticut, New York, Pennsylvania, North Carolina, Georgia, Delaware, South Carolina, and New Hampshire.)
- Only 24% of people knew the correct answer as to why the colonists fought the British (because of high taxes – taxation

without representation; because the British army stayed in their homes without permission and by force; and because they didn't have self-government).

This obvious lack of knowledge of history underscores the necessity to Embrace the Routines that give us the foundation of truth, especially when boosting creativity and innovation.

Embracing the Routine is my seventh superpower. It keeps the truth alive. And as an added benefit, it increases creativity and boosts innovation. As with the Olustee reenactors who polish their reenactment to be a little bit more accurate each year, creativity in a modern company today can be all about steadily changing things very, very gradually, so that those gradual shifts can become significant over the long run.

Instead of using creative problem solving to bring about some big change that disrupts everything right this minute (which most people fear), it can be about introducing small solutions, refining, and evolving your daily routines. This is where the power of using routines and slowly improving or embellishing them gradually creates creative and innovative change. When people hear this, the idea of creative problem solving becomes a lot less intimidating, and even welcoming.

In my consulting work, the term "innovation" is often used by leadership to induce great fear and anxiety in the front line. Most in leadership want innovation and can sometimes be insensitive to the very folks who are tasked with carrying it out, feeling that it is a sudden and dramatic event that is often feared by staff. So, the use of this seventh superpower gradually enables creative change in the organization and makes it organic in nature – it takes the fear, the sting, and the overwhelming sudden change out of innovation and makes it acceptable, repeatable, and even endorsable by all.

Embracing the Routine has become so much more important over the last few years as an anchor of truth, especially with everything going on in technology and the misinformation on social media. In your business or career, embracing routine and using this seventh superpower will uncover hidden truths about your product or service. This offers a reality to the customer who consumes them. Let's look at tool #1, which is Evolution, Not Revolution, to start to dig in and Embrace the Routine.

Tool #1: Evolution, Not Revolution

David Lee Edwards won the Powerball lottery in 2001. He won a staggering amount of money, which he had the option to accept as a lump sum, or in yearly annuity payments for 25 years. He won $73,000,000.00. And like just about every big lottery winner, he chose the lump sum, which came out to $41,000,000.00. Yet financial consultants[27] consistently warn that accepting the annuity payments is a far better option for the vast majority of lottery winners. Why?

Most people who win the lottery do not have stable financial structures, planning, discipline, and the know-how to manage a large sum of money. In order to successfully manage that type of award amount, most people need to have important structures in place to allow them to manage their windfall, like tax advisors, investment advisors, and budgetary restraints to make the winnings last as long as possible.

At the time of his winning, David had no job. He was recently fired from a telecommunications career and had needed money for back surgery. He had a 13-year-old Buick with 130,000 miles on it with a broken-down radiator that left him constantly stranded. He was on *Good Morning America*[28] shortly after winning and told the hosts that he was going to accept the lump sum because he felt that he could handle his own money just fine and considered the help of a financial advisor only hesitantly.

His first big move after accepting the $41-million–dollar lump sum was to spend one million dollars of it on cars, like a new Rolls Royce. He then spent $1.6 million on a house, $2 million on a private jet, and $4.5 million on failed businesses. All in all, David spent an eyewatering $3 million dollars in the first 90 days, and $12 million dollars in just the first year!

By 2006, just five years after winning the $41 million dollars, David was broke.[29] He died in a Kentucky storage unit where he was living, surrounded by dirty clothes and rotting food. He was just 58 years old.[30]

Roughly a third of lottery winners end up broke[31] just like David did. Lottery winners who accept the lump sum tend to spend it all recklessly with little regard to the future.

And that is where the tool of Evolution, Not Revolution comes in. When using this tool, it is all about evolving your business, career, product, or service over time – not revolutionizing everything all at once. It is all about accepting the annuity option of your winnings because, when using creativity and innovation in a solution-based mindset, it is truly like winning the lottery. Yet, it's not the state lottery you win; it's the lottery of opportunity and possibility.

Because David chose the big win up front, he couldn't keep up with all the rapid changes. And just like David, you have the choice of how you parse out creativity and innovation in everything that you do – and choosing a slow and deliberate pace is likely the most beneficial long-term path.

Taking the time that projects need in order to be successful and not just hammering past awaiting the next big deal is oftentimes the road of Evolution, Not Revolution. When we are able to slow down and become more accurate and beneficial, and show greater value to our clients or customers, we are in a better position to steadily do well over the long term. When we slow down and focus on doing some of the hard things at work, we are able to focus on the long-term benefits of problem solving, and not the short-term windfall of the latest and greatest.

One thing I see often is business people looking at any new tech – especially software – as some sort of goose that lays the golden egg of productivity and efficiency. The technology becomes a lot like the windfall from the lottery. A super concentrated burst of resources aimed to fix everything – now! This software, no matter what it costs, is exactly what my business needs right now!

Yet time and time, again rushing into the revolution and not embracing the evolution simply does not work. That software, after a while, isn't as powerful as you thought. That next round of seed money did not solve all the problems you ever had, like you thought it would.

Sometimes a new idea has to take hold suddenly and with swift and substantial changes, but I would argue that more often than not, taking time to implement little changes as you go along is more likely to be of benefit to you over the long run. For instance, if you need a new piece of equipment that has a significant cost, perhaps try to find a vendor who can supply the part at first. Or rent it. Just to see how it goes over the long run. If indeed it makes sense over time to buy the machine that makes the part, then that road can be crossed at a later time.

Far too often, we rush into things without slowly evolving our creative and innovative ideas because we want to see instant results, like a new lottery winner accepting a lump sum. But those supposedly instant results are not truly instantaneous. They take time, and in the end, the long game is what is important.

It's better to make investments that, over some time, evolve into a practical and useful pathway, an evolution not a revolution.

Embracing the Routine is all about evolution, not a sudden revolution. It is the small tasks that we make every day that eventually add up to significance. It is the steady approach we deliberately take to Embrace the Routine and live out changes in slow, considered, and impactful ways, with a dose of patience that is in such short supply these days.

That patience becomes its own measure of efficiency over time and is well worth the investment in Evolution, Not Revolution.

Tool #2: Define the Box

It is a popular myth that creativity and innovation come from an unbounded, unrestricted freedom.

Nothing could be further from the truth.

Most people think that creative problem solving is all about breaking free of the chains that hold us back. It's all about thinking outside of that famous box. But to truly tap into this kind of breakthrough innovation, you have to think inside the box by Defining the Box.

The box that we are perpetually trying to think outside of is the box we should be trying instead to define. The box gives us constraints on our creativity, and that is a good thing. A recent study published by the *Journal of Management*[32] has shown that managers can innovate better in their departments by embracing constraints instead of attempting to eliminate them to generate fresh ideas and creativity.

Fresh ideas and creativity can often be the key to a wildly successful company, product, or service and can be a major differentiator in a competitive advantage. And for many years, the prevalence of trying to eliminate all hurdles in order to create a safe space for innovation has caused creativity and innovation to not fully take root and be implemented in a risk-adverse and resource-constrained environment.[33] A far more predictable route to innovation is to embrace the constraints and innovate within the confines of those constraints to see a higher return on investment.

So how do we do this? How do we think inside the box and Define the Box in order to achieve greater innovative freedom? Here is a list of ways to Define the Box and to innovate within the constraints of the real world:

1. **Take Stock of What You Do Have.** Most people view whatever resources they may have in the dark of negativity instead of the light of positivity. You have the ability to choose how you view your constraints and make choices that are more creative. For example, the budget that you have for procuring that next great vendor for your department or company is lower than what the market has established. Here you have a choice: you can choose to either sulk or get creative. Perhaps a vendor from outside the industry that may not have experience in your field may work. When we take stock of what we have instead of looking at what we don't have, we Define the Box and recognize what tools we have and what tools we don't have. And in doing so, we give ourselves the permission to be creative and innovative, to come up with solutions to problems we are facing.

2. **Lower the Bar for Now.** If we have constraints of some sort, be they budgetary or schedule constraints or even resource or knowledge constraints, we can always lower the bar for now to get creative and innovative ideas flowing. We can always adjust the expectations of the goals to something more manageable and easy to obtain in the short run to gain momentum. For instance, there have been times in

my career as a keynote speaker that I have accepted invitations for speaking at conferences and companies for rates that were below my expectations. Now, you can look at this by saying that lowering the bar for your fee may not be the best thing to do, but I choose to look at it as a new opportunity for an industry I have yet to learn about or an association that could perhaps be a partner on several different educational events.

By lowering the bar temporarily, we may artificially support a goal that is not quite what we have strived to achieve, but hitting goals – any goals – makes people happy. And channeling that joy of accomplishment – however low it may be perceived – can always boost morale and allow for people to feel as if they are achieving success. Because they *are* achieving success.

When we build a sort of muscle memory of success and scale it to larger wins, it becomes easier because we remember how to do it. That way we further Define the Box with some specific, low-hanging goals that may not be what we first set out to achieve but will ultimately gain us some momentum on the road to bigger accomplishments. It turns out that if we lower the bar temporarily to allow success to happen sooner, sometimes we further Define the Box of what we view as success and allow ourselves a small taste of it.

3. **Eliminate Variety.** To help think inside the box and define it in order to achieve innovation or creativity, reduce variety.[34] A famous case study called the Jam Study[35] found that reducing choices of jam flavors led to better sales. When given the option to choose from 24 different varieties versus given the chance to buy only six varieties of jam, eight times more people would choose one of the six jams to buy. Focus on one singular goal instead of a whole host of goals to achieve. When we are constrained by circumstances that are outside

of our control, zooming into the single or select few may just be the way to Define the Box and come up with great innovations. When we remove the clutter of multiple goals on multiple deadlines, and instead focus on one or two things, we eliminate a variety of potential distractions that may pull us away from our goals and drive us into hyper-focused Solution Mindsets that execute that next big idea. Drastically reducing the variety of options can foster creativity and innovation by helping you Define the Box and embrace constraints, instead of being overwhelmed by too many goals.

The thought of embracing a routine to be more creative might seem counterintuitive. People might believe that thinking outside the box is where big ideas come from and what you should be aiming for to develop a more creative and innovative Solution Mindset.

But as you can see, that is often a false assumption.

Thinking inside the box is what we really should be doing to boost our problem-solving superpowers because thinking inside the box brings a whole host of improvements in innovation and creativity by setting constraints. Most people do better within a constraint-based environment – like the famous jam study. If we define the limitations, then we know what size box we happen to be in, and coming up with creative solutions in that box becomes more realistic. It's often not about earth-shattering ideas; it's about the gradual and steady implementation of creativity to keep truth alive.

Tool #3: Learn the Rules Before You Break Them

Caterpillar purchased another company called ERA in a merger in 2012,[36] the disastrous results of which are still being felt today.

Caterpillar is a US company focused on heavy equipment for the construction and mining industries, with a wide array of products from engines to bulldozers. ERA is a mining company in China focused on hydraulic roof supports for coal mines. On paper the deal looked amazing. Caterpillar looked to break all the rules by acquiring a company that gave them the ability to expand into the coal market in China.

Unfortunately, instead of first learning the rules and then breaking them to their advantage, Caterpillar made some dubious choices to break rules based on disrupting the system. The fact that ERA had poor accounting fidelity? No problem. Let's break the rules and proceed anyway. The fact that ERA's CEO was fired during the deal for honesty and transparency issues? No problem. Let's break the rules and proceed anyway. The due diligence that found ERA potentially floundering in a market they seemed to thrive in? No problem. Let's break the rules and proceed anyway.

To make matters even worse, Caterpillar relied heavily on advisors who were busy at the time accepting an award for a "cross-border deal of the year."[37] Asia's top bankers and Caterpillar associates gathered to celebrate the deal at the swanky awards gala and dinner celebration held at the Island Shangri-La in Hong Kong. Yep, everyone was in black tie that night. So what went wrong? How did Caterpillar not fully learn the rules before breaking them?

Understanding the existing framework of your product or service – or even your career – is essential to enhancing the creative and innovative potential of your ideas. But far too often, we are in such a rush to break the rules, or be a trailblazer, that we hurry to change things that we fail to fully comprehend in the first place. We don't learn all the rules, both about ourselves and any project we undertake, like a merger or acquisition. So, we change things for change's sake and run headlong into the future, only to wonder why we are not successful.

Caterpillar could have slowed the deal down, pumped the brakes, and learned a whole lot more about the rules in China before setting out to break them. For instance, they could have looked at the rules on accounting standards in China, which can sometimes leave a lot to be desired. It turns out that there are different accounting standards in China than there are in the US.[38] Knowing that would have perhaps led them to a different outcome. Or they could have looked into ERA's CEO and found rampant fraud and rule violations, and adjusted accordingly, but they did not.

Learning the rules is a critical part of breaking them. If we don't know what we are breaking in the first place, we can be reckless and make decisions that are at best uninformed, and at worst negligent. Caterpillar did not have all the facts; they didn't know all the rules of the game. Yet they insisted on breaking them with abandon in the name of progress and getting things done, and the results were catastrophic.

As a result of not learning the rules, Caterpillar had to take a $580 million dollar write-down[39] related to the merger. They had no new orders for hydraulic roof supports, and the number of working employees fell by at least a third one year after the deal ended.

Breaking the rules is a fine thing to do to usher in innovation, but not understanding fully what you are breaking in the first place is a risk that is unacceptable. In my consulting and keynote work, I often come across emerging leaders' groups or a professional accelerator that is designed to prepare the next generation for leadership tasks within certain industries. The groups and accelerators tend to gravitate toward my message of innovation and creativity, and rally around a Solution Mindset while looking at issues in their industries wholeheartedly, for which I am appreciative. But every so often I get a person in my mentorship work who is more interested in going scorched earth on the current practices of their industry without taking the time to learn why things are the way they are before changing them.

It is always a tricky situation. I am a proponent of change and an advocate of innovation and creativity in all levels of a business, but with that comes a great responsibility. And that responsibility is to learn what it is that you are trying to change before you do it. It is critical to learn the rules of the business, and moreover learn how those rules play out in reality because what you think may be enacted from the boardroom is not always what happens on the front line. So I encourage folks to really take the time to learn all the rules and understand them before strategically picking the ones to break, if at all.

Because getting it right is critical. And using my seventh superpower to usher in change by actually Embracing the Routine and looking for subtle opportunities is what ends up working year after year, time after time.

Conclusion

In this chapter we discovered my seventh superpower and all the ways we can Embrace the Routine to give us creative and innovative capabilities. We looked at Civil War reenactors and their preservation of truth; we examined corruption and its devastating effects on a Solution Mindset; and we looked at learning the rules before we break them. Now we explore superpower #8, which features the prisons in Norway and what we can learn from making mistakes. It may just surprise you to learn that mistakes can be one of the best things you can do on your journey to embracing your Solution Mindset.

8

Superpower #8: Fail Successfully

What Prison Reform in Norway Teaches Us About the Power of Making Mistakes

*I have not failed 10,000 times. I have successfully found
10,000 ways that will not work.*

—Thomas Edison

David Lee Windecher knows a thing or two about making a lot of mistakes in life. He was first arrested at age 11. He was caught shoplifting merchandise from a bicycle shop.[1] This was the first of his many mistakes to come. By the time he was 19, he had been arrested 12 more times. Burglary, robbery, larceny, DWI, loitering, possession.

Growing up poor in North Miami led David to desire things he wanted but could not afford – things that he felt could only be acquired by someone in his lot through criminal activity. He was angry that people had so much and that he and his family had so little. His father was an industrial machine painter and worked relentlessly – and was often treated unfairly by his employers – so David decided to take what he wanted any way he could. And that way led him down a dark road.

By middle school David was initiated into a local criminal street gang. That initiation consisted of him taking multiple beatings by the older members, falling, and then getting up again to take more. It gave him his street cred – a credibility that led to selling drugs.

By the time he was 16 he was a high school dropout and a seasoned, crafty, and smart criminal. He started his own faction and branched out to other forms of criminal activity including forging checks, stealing cars, and going on multistate runs to buy and sell drugs. Now his rap sheet featured aggravated battery, grand theft, and conspiracy. A litany of mistakes compounded by his desire to gain material wealth by any means necessary.

So, what became of David? Another young man lost to the system after making many compounding poor decisions leading to a life of mistake after mistake? You can certainly say that David headed down a pathway of failure like so many others, becoming yet another statistic in the criminal legal system, just like these shocking statistics below:

- The United States makes up about 5% of the world's population but has almost 25% of the world's incarcerated.[2]

- There are more Americans in prison today (approximately 2.3 million in 2018) than at any other time in US history even though crime rates are the lowest they have been since 1970.[3]

- In 2022, the last year we have data for, there are approximately 24,000 minors[4] in juvenile detention facilities.

One of the most important words commonly used in the corrections industry is *recidivism*, which is the tendency of a convicted criminal to reoffend and end up back in prison again and again.

In the United States, the rate of recidivism is 82%.[5] Meaning that 82% of people who get sent to prison once will reoffend within ten years and get sent back. An average of seven arrests for each person who winds up in the system. Fyodor Dostoevsky, the famous author of *Crime and Punishment*, once said, "A society should be judged not by how it treats its outstanding citizens but by how it treats its criminals." So how was David treated while incarcerated? Not very well. He was not rehabilitated, he was reenergized.

Soon, David was shaping up to be a typical product of the criminal legal system, in and out of custody, his recidivism rate very much in line with the national average. David's crime syndicate was getting more and more complex, and he was on a frightening path.

Yet he made a profound change.

Around the time of his last couple of arrests, he began to notice his family changing. His little brother was starting to sell drugs and carry guns just like he had. His sisters were dressed as gangbangers and starting to associate with some unsavory company. That's when he realized that he was headed down the wrong path, and after some divine intervention at church, he decided to turn his life around.

He was met with roadblock after roadblock. Try getting a job with a rap sheet like his. But he remembered that his father was treated poorly as a painter and never really had someone to advocate for him and others who were at the front line of the service industry. So, he got an idea: law school. Being a lawyer would help him advocate for those who couldn't advocate for themselves.

He finished his GED, attended local colleges, and after seven years of pursuing a bachelor's degree, finally graduated and became eligible for postgraduate studies. He applied to law schools across the country. But because of his rap sheet, he got accepted into only one. He quickly rose to the top of his class earning his juris doctorate degree and shortly after was sworn into the practice of law as his family looked on at the Miami-Dade County Courthouse, the very same courthouse where years earlier he wore an orange jumpsuit and faced serious criminal charges.

Today, he has a successful legal practice in Atlanta and is the founder of RED Foundation, which stands for Rehabilitation Enables Dreams. He actively looks for participants to mentor and gives leadership skills to enable rehabilitation in the truest sense of the word to help turn lives around, and stop the endless cycle of recidivism[6] once and for all. His basic premise is to see the good in everyone, no matter how many mistakes they make.

David's story is remarkable in that he took a bunch of mistakes and used them to form something both important and powerful. His mistakes give him that same street credibility that the initiation into gang life gave him, but now he is using the credibility to help others see their way out of constant recidivism. He made the choice to abandon crime and instead embrace law and order and accepted that the mistakes he made in the past led him to his own individual present today.

And that same story of making mistakes and yet still being able to turn them around can help you, too. Superpower #8 is all about learning how to Fail Successfully – because we all make mistakes. It's what we do with the mistakes we all make that really matters in the long run.

Companies make mistakes, too, not just people. Mercedes Benz famously purchased Chrysler for $30 billion dollars in the late 1990s only to lose $20 billion more when no one wanted to buy a Mercedes Benz–branded Chrysler,[7] among other really bad operational mistakes. Most of us are lucky enough to make mistakes that don't result in incarceration or the loss of billions of dollars. But some of us do make colossal mistakes. And that is what superpower #8 is all about – learning to Fail Successfully and rebound from all those mistakes that we will inevitably make.

And there is no better place to learn about mistakes – and how to Fail Successfully for our business and careers – than in the prison system in Norway.

Prison, Norway, and That Mistake Email You Sent

Today, many Norwegian prisons can be confused for hotels. But it wasn't always that way. The early 1990s saw Norway plagued with the same recidivism problems as the US. People would commit some sort of mistake, be put on trial, be judged guilty by the legal system, and then serve time in prison. After some point, they would be released only to offend again. Here's that word *recidivism* coming up again.

The concept of prisons is at least 4,000 years old.[8] They existed in ancient Mesopotamia as a way to deal with people who offended the law but could not be instantly executed. Pretty much every mistake was met with capital punishment back in the day. Adultery or breaking the Sabbath or theft were all met the same way: capital punishment. But early societies, especially in America,[9] decided that they would be killing an awful lot of folks for seemingly minor violations. There had to be a better way.

So they began to moderate the approach. The old thinking that capital punishment was the only treatment for every person's mistake gave way to other types of punishments. Other punishments deemed worthy at the time were punishments like whipping or branding – not much better, but at least a start. Note that in all these cases, punishment, not rehabilitation, was the goal.

But crimes kept happening. And mistakes kept getting made by society.

So authorities developed new methods of punishment. In the 16 and 17th centuries, banishment became popular again after a long hiatus from biblical times. The concept is pretty simple – people would be sent to live away from the rest of society, and good luck to them! The common logic of the time was that the pesky prisoner problem was gone. For a while, Britain was sending its convicts to the United States as a form of banishment punishment, but after the colonies gained independence from the British in 1776, the English sent all their convicts to Australia.[10]

Again and again throughout time, the emphasis was on punishment and not rehabilitation. And the modern system in the United States is not much different, although as we saw earlier there are valiant efforts like David Windecher's RED program, which is so effective at stopping the cycle of recidivism in the criminal justice system. But I wanted to find somewhere in the world where the actual justice system itself was focused on rehabilitation instead of punishment, because there is a direct correlation between rehabilitation and superpower #8 Fail Successfully, and my research led to the prisons of Norway.

Norway decided in the late 1990s to mend their prisons with a move away from punishment and toward rehabilitation.[11] That simple shift of focus has led to remarkable results that began with the infrastructure of their prison system.[12] Norway has 57 prisons spread throughout the country. At first that may sound like a lot, but these are completely different from the prisons in the United States. For one, they are all smaller prisons – the largest has 400 cells while most average around 70 cells. They are not built in faraway locations; they are right inside communities and integrated into society. The system is focused on rehabilitation in three unique milestones:[13]

1. **The First Milestone Is Called "Normality."** Normality deals with removing the stigma of the offender and dictates that life behind bars must mirror as close as possible to normal life outside of prison. Even in the most extreme offenses like murder, Norway's system is still focused on normalizing the integration of the offender back into everyday society while in prison by allowing the prisoner to play sports, take classes, cook, and live largely unimpeded by security officers.

2. **The Second Milestone Is Called "Progression."** This milestone deals with preparing people while they are still in prison for life on the outside. Progression allows for offenders to earn more and more freedoms by completing certificates, taking on responsibilities or accomplishing goals inside of prison. As their sentences near an end,[14] family visitations and even going home to live for a few days a month, become commonplace. This second phase aims to help released prisoners become better neighbors, stop recidivism, and help better integrate released offenders.

3. **The Third and Final Milestone Is Called "Dynamic Security."**[15] Dynamic security focuses on the role of the prison employees, the guards, the officers, and other prison staff. They interact with prisoners on a personal level. Playing card games, sharing meals together, and even helping inmates talk through issues they may be having. It's a shift in mentality from barriers and regimented security of, let's say, a Salvadoran prison,[16] to an openness and mutual respect. It also allows officers to be better equipped to handle issues when they do arise because they know the inmates on a more

personal level. Guards in Norway even tell stories[17] of seeing inmates outside the prison thanking the guards for how they were treated while incarcerated.

The whole point of the prison system in Norway (and some Scandinavian countries by extension) is to rehabilitate and not to punish. Imagine if we tried that here in the US. Might that work for us too?

And that got me thinking a lot about what would happen if we were to try looking at our mistakes at work the same way. Instead of looking to punish mercilessly the offender in the workplace, we would look toward solutions to rehabilitate the mistake. What would we do differently if we were the ones who committed the mistake? Remember it's not a matter of if, but a matter of when. We all make mistakes. So can we take the lessons learned by Norway's prison system and apply them to our workplace instead?

The answer is a resounding yes. In a world full of mistakes at work, we can be so hard on ourselves. Yes, I know that when we make mistakes at work they are often not elevated to civil or criminal crimes, but they are mistakes after all, and we treat ourselves as if we have committed some capital offense and we punish ourselves – vowing to never ever make that mistake again. We feel embarrassed and often try to cover up the mistake as quickly as possible to move on in hopes that no one noticed.

Yet I wonder if this is the wrong way to look at mistakes at work.

Perhaps this brief look at crime and punishment both in the US and abroad can help us appreciate different ways of looking at mistakes and give us a Solution Mindset for handling mistakes. Instead of sweeping our mistakes under the rug and vehemently denying they were ever made, which is what most people do with mistakes at work, maybe we can process and learn from our mistakes. What would happen if we could learn from the Norwegian prison system and institute a system of reform for mistakes at work to transform these mistakes into a superpower by learning how to Fail Successfully? We could start by creating a mini-manifesto, which would have the following three steps that would help us deal with mistakes made at work and ultimately give us a resulting superpower – the ability to Fail Successfully:

1. **Admit the Mistake.** No one ever went to prison for cc'ing all, in an email, by mistake, the company's monthly financials. (Yep, that one was me. I made that mistake once.) Is that a careless mistake, sure. I was rushed and I was trying to keep up with some crazy deadline and – whoops – I sent an email that went to everyone that should not have been sent. Should I have been punished for it? Any punishment doled out would have paled in comparison to how hard I was on myself. I accepted and admitted the mistake. Yet what I learned by admitting the mistake was far more powerful than the mistake in the first place.

   I sent another email right away saying that I made a mistake by sending that email and to please delete the previous email. I learned that most people – not all – deleted the mistake email right away. Some even told me that they too got close to making that same "cc everyone" mistake and shared a bit of empathy with me. Some were downright horrible about it and didn't include me on emails for a while because they deemed me a "security risk." But you know what ended up happening? A whole lot of nothing. I was anxious and afraid that everything would go haywire and I would get fired, but that never materialized. Instead of punishment, I found rehabilitation.

   Time healed this particular wound, and I eventually figured out that putting a Post-it by my computer screen that said "check the CC" stopped the mistake from happening again. So, this mistake was little punished other than some bruised ego on my part and a few staff giving me a cold shoulder for a while. And the rehabilitation made me think a bit more before hitting send on emails, allowing for the kind of rehabilitation that enabled me not only to learn from the mistake but turn it into Failing Successfully. I haven't cc'ed all since then.

2. **Analyze the Mistake.** No one sets out to purposefully make a mistake (well most people don't) and so most people don't want to take the time to learn from them because it is inconvenient, embarrassing, or uncomfortable. When a mistake happens, it can also be the worst possible timing ever. Who wants to take some time out to learn and rehabilitate when the company's financials have been inadvertently sent out to the wrong people? But I argue that if we don't take the time out at exactly when the mistake happens – however inconvenient – we cannot learn from it. Don't rush to clean up your mistake or pretend it never happened. Take some time. Look at what happened. Make a list of things that led to the mistake happening, and then make a list of things that you can do to address the mistake in the first place. Why did it happen in the first place? Are there safeguards that can be put in place to prevent the next mistake from happening? Is it instead a blessing in disguise like most mistakes at work end up being? We don't want to deprive ourselves of a learning opportunity that analyzing the mistake offers us.

3. **The Sweet Spot.** Obsessing and dwelling over the mistake is not good. But neither is quickly moving on and not acknowledging the mistake in the first place. There is a sweet spot somewhere in between that is different for everyone, and learning to identify that sweet spot for yourself is essential. It

is the zone between punishment and rehabilitation that you need to find for yourself, depending on the severity and scope of the mistake. That zone is where the learning happens. For instance, if your mistake is missing a deadline at work for a particular project, it will probably be inappropriate to quit promptly and never deliver a project again. But it would also be inappropriate to quickly move on not acknowledging the mistake at all and forget about it. The key is balance; the ability to determine the right balance of punishment will lead to the correct rehabilitation. You may have some external factor like a boss or a market that punishes you, or it may be a personal punishment. Yet in both cases balancing the punishment with rehabilitation and finding that sweet spot so that you learn but not dwell on the mistake can yield great results in transforming that mistake into Failing Successfully.

This type of mini-manifesto can give us wonderful opportunities to turn the mistakes we make at work into Failing Successfully. Yet we need some more tools to help us Fail Successfully because while everyone in the world wants to talk about success, few want to spend time talking about failure. And that is a mistake. Because failure – if done successfully – can be one of the most powerful superpowers from *The Solution Mindset* that will allow you to thrive. Let's dive into tool #1, which deals with life without regrets.

Tool #1: Live Without Regrets

Regret is one of the biggest poisons we carry as human beings. It is driven by fear. When our fear of making mistakes prevents us from trying things that we want to do, that's when regret can creep in. The interesting thing about regret is that it is mostly cumulative. It takes several regrets to add up before you are even aware of the fact that you have them. At work, we get caught up in an endless cycle of "if only" thinking and soon it's the only thing we can think about.

Regret rarely shows up after one thing. It's not something that pops up when we – for example – pass on that coworker gathering we were invited to or decide not to work a bit harder on the presentation for the big new sale. It pops up when we add several of these decisions together and suddenly get blindsided with the realization that we regret not having pushed a bit harder on that presentation or gotten out of our comfort zone to attend that coworker gathering.

Regret gets worse. We tend to regret things more when we see that the outcome we missed was successful and we think to ourselves "if only" I would have participated. "If only" I would have gotten in there earlier. "If only" I would have jumped out in time. We tend to blame ourselves and regret not taking a different course of action when in reality there is no way we could have known in the first place what the outcome would have been.

I see this quite a bit in the financial services industry work that I do. It is not surprising to see folks kicking themselves for feeling as if they missed that security purchase or missed that latest investment. They only feel that way because in hindsight they saw the investment do well, and now they feel as if they should have participated.

The interesting thing is that no one ever feels regret over the opportunities they missed that didn't pan out successfully! No one ever kicks themselves in regret for not having invested in that particular investment that tanked, bombed, and ultimately failed.

So, what can we do? Is there a better way to deal with regret so that we can embrace superpower #8 and Fail Successfully? You bet. Here are some things that will push down the poison of regret to allow mistakes and know, deep down within our soul, that even if we fail (and we are likely to), we had the creative initiative to try:

1. **Ask for That Raise. Today.** One of the most common regrets that people have in the workplace is not asking for a raise. A recent study has shown that 60%[18] of people at work regret not asking for a raise sooner or even not asking for a raise at all. This also is the same regret that businesses have when their price stagnates for their product or service, and they do not try to revive their pricing strategy accordingly. The time for that is today. Regret will rear its ugly head if you don't try. And not trying is the exact thing that causes the regret in the first place. It is driven by fear of making mistakes. We are afraid that we will upset our boss by asking for a raise. Or we are afraid that we will upset customers by implementing that price increase. We fear that we will lose our job if we ask for that raise. Or we fear that the customer will go to a competitor, and we will lose out by raising prices.

   The thing is that we cannot Fail Successfully if our fear of regret and failure prevents us from trying in the first place. That is why I recommend starting today. Creep up those prices for your product or service. Ask your boss for a raise. Now take a deep breath: the world has not come to an end! Maybe you will get that raise, maybe you won't. Maybe your boss doesn't fully recognize your worth, or maybe you will get the raise and feel better about the whole thing. On the business side, you may lose a few customers – or they may not even notice. You can always go back to the original prices and package them at a discount, turning the mistake into a win for your customers. The point in both cases is simply this: if we are guided by regret, we will never be able to live The Solution Mindset and come up with novel problem-solving abilities at work. We will let fear rule our decision-making and in that fear, there is never any creative or innovative advancement. Each mistake is an opportunity to grow and move forward.

David Windecher, from our chapter's opening story, could have regretted his criminal history and done nothing, sulking at the fact that no one will ever hire a convict – and moreover – no one will ever give a convict an education in the legal system to become a lawyer. But he forged forward without succumbing to regret and was able to accomplish goals that most people would consider a long shot. But David is not most people, and neither are you.

2. **Recognize That It's Not Too Late.** One of the most toxic things about regret is the feeling that it is all too late and we have missed the boat. Regret makes us feel as if there is no point in trying anyway. Yet that is the furthest thing from the truth. It is indeed not too late – and not only that, you can overcome whatever regret is holding you back. The very feeling that it is too late is drawn from a well of fear. It's the same fear that drives us not to try new things when looking to problem solve at work because the fear of making mistakes leads us to feel as if it's too late. We already had the opportunity pass. There is nothing we can do. These reactions are all categorically false, and instead of believing that is it too late, recognizing that it is not too late will help you to spur that next big idea.

Most people think that start-ups and other businesses are started and run by people much younger and that they are too late to get in the game. Yet almost a third of new start-ups are run by people over 40![19] Think of something that you may feel you were too late on. Is it speaking up in that meeting and saying that perfect thing to the client? Or perhaps it is the fear that you didn't pick up that new work skill that seemed great at the time yet you let it pass you by. Or maybe you feel it's too late to start that business. In all cases, feeling like you have missed that moment is no reason not to start now. It's never too late. The feeling that we missed out and we are too late is just another manifestation of regret. It's fear. And the finest antidote to that fear is shaking off the chains and trying what we thought we were too late for in the first place.

Regret is a nasty thing we do to ourselves. Yet you can overcome regret simply by trying to do the things that you regret not doing. And in doing so – sure – there may be failure. Heck – there most likely will be failure. But not trying and not learning from these mistakes will prevent you from finding a repeatable and sustainable way to Fail Successfully. And learning how to Fail Successfully may be one of the most important things you can ever do for your business or career.

Tool #2: Fail Fast and Fail Often

Creativity and innovation are iterative tools that are built on the heaps and heaps (mountains really) of failures. No one gets it right the first time, so failing more can be better for your career and life. Like a muscle that gets used over and over again, failing becomes part of the process and not something to be feared. Fail Fast and Fail Often through The Solution Mindset lens becomes an approach of rapidly testing ideas and expecting them to fail. You get ideas out into the world to be tested in small chunks, small pieces, and little focused instances to see if what you think may be a great idea is actually working. Then accepting failure, learning from it, and moving on. Quickly.

The main thing to remember when using the Fail Fast and Fail Often tool is that whatever you are testing is designed, from the start, to fail. The test is made to crash and burn, not to succeed. And in doing so, it takes the sting out of having to be successful all the time and instead allows for failure, which breeds learning and finally another solution.

For example, Thomas Edison failed many, many times in making a lightbulb filament.[20] He and his team notoriously tried material after material to get the filament to glow just right and for the length of time needed until they stumbled on the correct one. It took many failures to get it right, and when the failure proved that the particular material used did not work, the team moved on to the next one. In other words, they failed fast and often, then intelligently deduced the next material to test based on the failures of the past.

Edison and his team didn't dwell on mistakes. They didn't think about all the money they lost by failing, they didn't think about how horrible their research and development was, nor did they beat themselves up for not coming up with the correct filament even though they were the experts in the field. They failed fast, failed often, intelligently deduced the next step, and moved on. So, what can you do to Fail Fast and Fail Often? Here are the steps you can use to fail fast and learn, then move on to the next failure to emerge just a bit more intelligent than you were at the start:

1. **Tiny Task, Hyperfocus Launch.** Find something in your business or career that needs to be changed or something that needs to be updated, refreshed, or otherwise innovated. It may be a new market that you want to break into, it may be a new résumé that you want to craft to change jobs, it may be a new and different customer base you'd like to pursue. Identify what you would like to test and now break it up into a tiny task. For instance, if you're thinking of changing up

your résumé because you want to go after a different job than you have now, then try the new résumé only on two leads. If you are trying to break into that new market, pick one tiny segment of it. If you are trying to pursue a different customer base, then hyperfocus on only three. Now launch the test. Get it out there into the real world. This is about trying your test on a tiny goal, because don't forget you are after all expecting to (mostly) fail.

2. **Find the Lesson.** Now that you put a test out there, and you are hyper-focused on a tiny portion of a test field, the failures will begin to come in! And here is where you have an important choice to make. You either accept the failure and look intelligently for the lesson in it, or you choose not to and get deflated and give up. It's a simple choice really, and I hope that the choice you end up making is to accept the failure, Fail Successfully and intelligently. Look shrewdly for trends in the failure and see what it may be telling you. Sometimes there is no trend, there is a single point of failure that you must learn from. So, find the lesson and learn from it.

3. **Tweak Slightly Based on the Lesson.** This is the point where the failure has come in, you have gleaned some kind of knowledge and you may be asking yourself – ok – now what? This step is all about using that lesson learned intelligently. In the case of the résumé, it may be a recruiter that has called you to tell you that you didn't receive a job offer, so you may want to change a few lines here and there on your résumé based on the new intel before getting it out again. In the case of trying to pursue the different customer base, this may be the initial reports that the customer base is using a competitor's software that they are accustomed to. So you may want to tweak your offering based on this new intel to be more acceptable to that new customer, and try again. In

the case of the new market, it may be feedback coming in that the market is already saturated. So you may want to change your offering based on the new intel so that the market can see some differentiator, and try again. That is really the point of where the fun begins. How you tweak, how you edit, how you reposition, and how you adapt is the secret sauce of Fail Fast and Fail Often. How you do it is up to you. Remember, it is ok to fail. It's expected. So the pressure of getting the modifications "right" is low. Just keep trying. Take the feedback, add your intelligence to it, and change it slightly based on the lesson that has come in, then go to step #4.

4. **Rinse and Repeat.** Step #4 is all about going back to step #1 armed with the following:

   - You hyper-focused a tiny test you deem worthy.
   - It failed.
   - You got some feedback and gained intelligence from it.
   - You tweaked based on the feedback thoughtfully and intelligently.
   - You try again.

Fail Fast and Fail Often in a Solution Mindset allows you to take all the pressure off having to get it right and allows you to get it wrong. When you feel little or no pressure to get it right then you allow for feedback to come in and intelligently adjust until one shining day when the adjustment is just enough, the tweak is just profound enough, the alteration just right, it will make the venture truly shine. Don't give up. Don't quit. Keep editing until you end up with the right fit.

Tool #3: Slow Overnight Success

Unfortunately, our society worships instant success. We love to hear about the company who sells out worldwide on their very first product launch. Or the author who hit the bestseller list on their first week! But the truth is that this rarely happens. True success takes a long time. And overnight success comes slowly over a long period of time with sustained effort. But most of all, it comes with learning how to Fail Successfully over the long haul. Failing and then learning from your failures to grow into eventual success.

Tool #3 Slow Overnight Success deals with the long game. Behind every bestselling book is an author or influencer on YouTube who has spent years researching their ideas and building their audience. Behind every new product launch are countless hours (sometimes years) of research that position the brand to succeed in what appears to be overnight success, but what is in reality Slow Overnight Success.

To the outside, it seems like an overnight success but for people who worked on it, it's a slow, slow build with many mistakes made along the way. Even if they don't want to share that part with you. The race is not for the swift, but for those who endure. The mistakes you make along the way will become a badge of honor and vital experience picked up along the way.

There are two central points that have to do with making Slow Overnight Success happen for you in your career or business:

1. **Mistakes Can Be Opportunities You Never Knew You Needed.** Since all of us at some point will make mistakes, what results from the mistakes may surprise you. You have embraced Fail Fast and Fail Often and have evolved your mistakes with intelligent learning at every turn with tool #2 of the Fail Successfully superpower. You have dedicated to Live Without Regrets by asking for what you need now and not waiting until tomorrow with tool #1 of the Fail Successfully superpower. Now you need another tool to help you understand that sometimes mistakes can be opportunities

that you never knew you needed. Mistakes can essentially be a vessel to new and uncharted lands. They can be the entry point to a direction that you have never before considered. When we view our mistakes with intelligence and we look at how and why the mistake occurred, we may find absolute confusion in the result. We may find that the result of the mistake is the furthest thing from what we thought would happen. But sometimes, mistakes lead to a path never before imagined.

For example, Rovio, the maker of the famous game Angry Birds, had notoriously suffered more than 50 failed games on the market that had flopped in unexpected ways.[21] Angry Birds was their fifty-first release and a game that was born out of 50 previous mistakes. No one at Rovio ever set out to design Angry Birds, it literally came from 50 other mistakes that became an opportunity that Rovio never knew they needed, and since has proven to be one of the most successful video games of all time.[22] All this happened by realizing a mistake that became an opportunity they never knew that they needed. And since mistakes abound all around us each day, sometimes they can take us places we never imaged if we are able to view mistakes as potential new paths for us to pursue. It takes a bit of creative thinking and a Solution Mindset to be able to see an opportunity leading somewhere as most people would never have seen – and it may lead to new and uncharted waters of great creative and innovative success.

2. **Don't Be Afraid to Show the Mess.** Often, making mistakes is messy. ~~Yset~~ Yet the first thing we do when we make a mistake is try to hide it. We shelter it from prying eyes, afraid of what the world would think of us when we make mistakes. But sometimes the ~~bet~~ best things that happen when we make mistakes is the embrace of Slow Overnight Success that leads

to new opportunities. Instead of covering our tracks and presenting ourselves as geniuses, ~~lets us~~ let's show the mistakes. For instance, take this section of my book and look at all the markup my editor Kelly Talbot from Wiley made. It's like a bloodbath of edits that I could take in one of ~~to~~ two ways: Either I could think that I'm a horrible writer (which just may be the case), or I could think that the writing process, much like launching a business or the trajectory of a truly great career, is messy. That mess is part of the secret sauce of success. Just as the exposed edits of this section show all the mistakes I made along the way, and perhaps I have made more mistakes than other writers, the point is that the final product – the rest of this book outside this section – is always a more cleaned-up version of the mess that it takes to get there in the first place. And not ~~beeing~~ being afraid to show the messy parts may liberate you from the fear of making the mistake in the first place, which in turn will help you Fail Successfully.

Because there is no such thing as overnight success, looking at success as a slow process designed for the long game will allow us to take our cumulative failures and learn to how Fail Successfully. Although the overnight success happens very rarely (some people do win the lottery, however minuscule that population is), we shouldn't use it as the baseline to define our success.

Conclusion

In this chapter we learned about the eighth superpower and the ways we can Fail Successfully. We reviewed David's incredible story of redemption and his dedication to reduce recidivism with his incredible RED Foundation, we looked at the video game Angry Birds and saw that success just may come after unexpected failures and the lessons they teach, and finally we learned how to Fail Successfully and fully embrace the eighth superpower of The Solution Mindset. Now we explore super-power #9 Question the Data, which will teach us how to use creativity and innovation to question metrics and use data in a real and deliberate way, different from what is convention-ally taught and understood, to enable ourselves to fully embrace The Solution Mindset.

9

Superpower #9: Question the Data

What Global Population Growth Teaches Us About Understanding Metrics

There are three kinds of lies: lies, damn lies, and statistics.
—Mark Twain

We hear dire news all the time. And it has a profound influence on us. News that feels incredibly powerful – as if the whole world is in imminent danger. Moreover, we hear it repeated from a variety of sources, be it social media, the news, friends and family, and others. We feel hopeless as this news is seldom good news. It is always bad. It is always some kind of circumstance that tells a tale as old as time: humans exploiting whatever it is, fill in the blank, for the benefit of just a few.

Like a conspiracy that catches and fails to let go, the scapegoat always is the other: be it the other country, the other people, or the other religion.

The bad news is always set in the loftiest of hyperbole. It is always dire. Take for instance the recent news on overpopulation in the world. It has been continuously discussed for over 10 years now. Like a cancer that won't go away. The cycle has been familiar: dire, hopeless, huge in scope, out of reach, and beyond anyone's redemption. The scapegoat in this case is people who have kids. We are just having too many children that the earth cannot contain, and that is the news we are blasted with.

The news goes on to tell us that overpopulation is a huge problem on earth. It took one hundred and fifty years for the world's population to go from one million to three million, but it only took 12 years to go from 7 billion to 8 billion.[1] At that exponential rate of growth, we'll see the earth reach the maximum capacity of the number of people it can hold in most of our lifetimes.

Like a scene out of Mad Max, there will inevitably be a world war over resources. There will be too many dang humans around, and they will have to fight for every single thing. There will be no trees left. No water to drink. No place to live. There will be no hope for humanity, and we will end up self-imploding, going the way of the dinosaurs on this short road to extinction.

This overpopulation dissemination is the ideology of antihumanism.[2] And it can be found in anything from overpopulation to politics. What this basically means is a complete opposite view of this book: Antihumanist preachers believe that people are essentially vermin – parasitic and destructive. In their view, humans will spread unchecked across the globe, driven by selfish ambitions that destroy, annihilate, and overpopulate without restraint. They need to be stopped by some benevolent power (usually the person who is peddling this bad news), which of course is never clearly defined yet used as a weapon under the pretense of the antihumanists being more civilized, more cultured, and far better educated than all the rest of us. So therefore they know better what's good for us than we know ourselves.

So yes, overpopulation is clearly a problem. Or is it? Are the Antihumanists right?

If you look beyond all the doom and gloom, you will find the truth. And the truth matters today more than ever. Because in a world where people weaponize the facts and data for their own agendas (in the case of antihumanism, it's an agenda of self-detestation) the actual truth is that the world's population is falling. Not growing but falling! Take a look at these facts that are seldom repeated:

- According to an article in *The Economist*, "In 2000 the world's fertility rate was 2.7 births per woman . . . Today it is 2.3 and falling."[3]

- The largest 15 countries by GDP all have a fertility rate below the replacement rate. Below the replacement rate means that people aren't having enough kids to keep up with people who are dying. That includes the United States, but also China and India who together account for more than a third of the global population.[4]

- By 2100, most major economies will fall 20–50% as there will be not enough people around to replace those who die. Think about that for a second. All this because the fertility rate drops below the replacement rate.[5]

- Age structures are inverting – meaning that the number of older people continue to grow while the number of younger people continue to shrink.[6]

How do we get from the world being overpopulated in our lifetime to a slow decline of the earth's population? How do we get to the truth of data when it is being weaponized by a select few? We are told that the data is infallible, watertight, and fool-proof. But we must use my ninth superpower – Question the Data – in order to find the truth.

Four Filters for Sifting Data

My ninth superpower is all about Questioning the Data no matter what the data is – be it data about the earth or data about the third-quarter financials – and making an educated decision on whether to act on that data or not. The educated decision part takes some work: It is part skepticism, part reading up, part history, part detective work, and all creativity and innovation fueled. It is a conditional state in which any data that is being received is driven through filters before it passes muster. Here is the litmus test for any data you receive with some pretty easy-to-follow steps – and these four filters will work for you both on the job and beyond:

1. **Skepticism.** The only time you will see a skeptical approach in this book is in regard to superpower #9 Question the Data. As you know, positivity is one of the most important things you can do to harness your Solution Mindset. It's a corner-stone of The Solution Mindset. But not when it comes to data. When it comes to data, be mercilessly skeptical. For instance, if you hear doom and gloom stories of overpopula-tion choking the world of all hope, your first reaction should be skepticism. Ask yourself the following questions: Where is this data coming from? Who's agenda does it forward? What do they have to gain by inducing panic? Likewise, when you see a report at work of the latest financials, or when you see

the latest PR piece go out at the office, you ask the very same questions. Be skeptical. When we look at the data with prying eyes, we can begin to uncover the hidden narrative that separates fact from fiction.

2. **Read More Classics.** Let's say you are interested in American politics or history. And in any given year, you hear the news is saying that the sky is falling in America. Is that really going on? You may think from hearing these things that our republic is in unprecedented peril, but if you read more classics then you know that this supposed "data" of imminent collapse is not true. How do you know for certain? You read more classics. Any interest in American politics would drive you to educate yourself on the classics. Read the Constitution and all the amendments (the first 10 known as the Bill of Rights). It's available in any library and free online. Then you may read John Locke's *Two Treatises of Government*,[7] the first line of which was written in 1689 still stirs the soul today: *"Slavery is so vile and miserable an estate of man, and so directly opposite to the generous Temper and Courage of our Nation."* It's available online for free, check for the link in the footnotes. In it John Locke attacks patriarchy and pushes for a more civilized society based on natural laws and contract theory. The book is a key foundational text in classic liberalism and is one of the foundations of the US republic. Reading it makes you more educated and gives you context on all the doom and gloom we are hearing about today on the news. Or read David Hume's *A Treatise on Human Nature*, written in 1738 when he was just 28 years old,[8] on how desire rather than reason governs human nature. Why is it important to read these old books? These are the books that our Founding Fathers – the framers of the Constitution – widely read. They act as an anchor to understanding the chaos

going on in the world today and give you context for all the demagogues (more to follow in tool #2) out there hawking news with no context. These books have a hidden benefit as well: they teach you how to think of data both at work and beyond. Read Plato's *The Republic* or even *The Trial of Socrates* to assemble knowledge on American politics and history.

The next time you hear the sky is falling, the classics will give you comfort in understanding the underpinnings of Western thought. And in them you will find the truth on the data being bent for nefarious purpose every day. By reading more classics you derive context on the situation, context that will allow you to use historical data to question the reporting of today's so-called "facts."

3. **Athens and Jerusalem.** Another crucial aspect of questioning data involves looking to both Athens and Jerusalem. Much of Western thought draws on two complementary traditions: the reason of Athens and the moral insight of Jerusalem. Athens gave us some of the greatest minds in human history, shaping the tools of rational thinking and critical analysis. Jerusalem, in turn, contributed the moral and ethical frameworks that guide our sense of right and wrong.

When we combine the clarity of reason with the guidance of morality, we approach the highest human achievement: the pursuit of wisdom. Questioning data effectively requires both – reason helps us separate emotion from judgment, while morality ensures that our decisions are ethically sound. Neither alone is sufficient; together, they provide a full lens through which to analyze, understand, and solve problems. Like two sides of the same coin, ethics and reason work hand in hand to guide us toward thoughtful, responsible action.

Take CEO Elizabeth Holmes at her company Theranos for example.[9] She violated a bunch of moral codes but did not violate reason – indeed it was reason that led her to make huge sums of money and become the buzz of Silicon Valley! But her violation of the moral code ultimately sent her to jail. You cannot have one without the other. Combining both reason and morality allows us to Question the Data correctly and in balance. Because when reason is always weighed against a moral core, decisions become anchored in a forever balanced quest for wisdom. And finding truth within the data becomes a viable goal.

4. **Detective Work.** Now that you have had a high dose of skepticism and you read and reread the classics and you understand morality and reason's balance, do a bit of detective work on the data that others seem to think is infallible. I'll give you an example.

Perhaps you are in the retail business, and you see that store sales for a location in Des Moines are off the charts. It is much higher than your company's similar stores with the same square footage in comparable markets. Your first instinct may be to make that store a model – as it is so successful! But then you remember Nir's four-step plan to analyze the data. You begin by being skeptical. Is there an error in reporting? What's going on with this store that is not happening in nearby markets? Is this some kind of anomaly in reporting? Good! You are already following the procedure to making an educated decision on whether to act on that data or not.

The classics have been read and you have trained yourself on how to think about data in a new and different way. Now you balance reason with integrity and you uncover some facts that are beyond the spreadsheet: this store has high sales, sure, but the staff is miserable, and there are high employee turnover rates. You also uncover the truth: this is a bubble, not a sustainable model. How do you know it's a bubble? More detective work shows a nearby store, which is your only competitor, has temporarily shut its doors for a remodel and customers have no other option than to shop at your store. For now. By looking at only the data, you would have missed the reality of what is really going on. Question the Data. It will not only make you a better citizen but a better steward of your business or career.

When we're constantly being bombarded by so much misinformation, being able to Question the Data allows you to examine the so-called "facts" in a way that brings honesty and integrity to light. It is your duty as a citizen of the planet Earth to use your Solution Mindset to not accept information on faith without questioning the source and running it through the four filters. That very questioning of the source is what will enable you to solve any problem at work. And it will also enable you to solve any problem on Earth like the ones discussed in earlier chapters where Titouan is healing reefs and David is revolutionizing recidivism and Gil is empowering people with disabilities.

By looking at what the true metrics are, you ensure you aren't being manipulated by overinflated numbers or convincing emotional stories. With the hard facts at your disposal, you radiate integrity – and therefore are in a better position to build creative and innovative solutions that actually work.

The Man Who Flew Too Much

The story of Steven Rothstein starts with an amazing year at work. In 1987, as a stockbroker in Chicago, he was having the kind of year that many of us dream about. Hitting goal after goal led him to a windfall and the ability to purchase something so transformative, so incredible, that it would change his life forever.

Instead of buying a fancy boat or a bigger house with his windfall from work, Steven purchased an American Airlines lifetime pass called the AAirpass that was being sold at the time for $250,000 ($694,553 in today's dollars adjusted for inflation).

What is the AAirpass? American Airlines offered the AAirpass based on data that was supposed to be infallible, foolproof, and trustworthy. And what ended up happening was anything but. American Airlines executives had a great idea – they were going to come up with some super-inflated astronomical high price for a first-class ticket. To sweeten the deal on this super high-priced ticket, it could be used over and over again – no matter how many times the person wanted to fly – each time for a first-class seat. And to further entice people to buy it – they could also fly wherever they wanted, whenever they wanted. For life. First-class ticket to Paris? Check. First-class ticket to New York from Dallas? Sure thing. All one price paid once up front, for a lifetime of use.[10]

Deregulation had hit the airlines hard, and they needed to inject some cash into the operation as quickly as possible. The data was pored over. It showed that the executives were on to a great idea. Here is a small fraction of what the data looked like that led to the decision to implement the AAirpass:

- The data showed that if the price was high enough (and $250,000 was high enough), it would be profitable because someone just cannot fly enough to recoup that investment.

- The data showed that anyone who could afford it was not a "frequent traveler" of the airline – and moreover showed that anyone who could afford a quarter million dollars had access to private aviation that they would use instead of commercial flights.

- The data showed that the injection of cash would be good for the airline and enable them to make it through the tumults of deregulation.

And so based on these data, executives at American Airlines rolled out the program. Steven Rothstein was one of the very first to sign up. And he used every single privilege that the pass would give him. Extensively. He even purchased the accompanying companion pass for $150,000 and was able to take his family on trips with him. His daughter[11] had visited almost all 50 states by the time she was 11, and weekends in Tokyo or family trips to Australia or India or Israel became commonplace. The reality was that Steven and others who purchased the AAirpass simply flew too much.[12] Across a 25-year period, Steven booked 1,000 first-class flights. In total, he flew more than 30 million miles.[13]

But the good times were coming to a screeching halt.

The data ended up being wrong. Very wrong. So wrong in fact that American Airlines began an investigation in 2007 into the most prolific users of the AAirpass. Steven was one of them that they investigated. They found that he cost the airlines a reported $21 million in ticket fees that they could have made had they sold the seat to someone else.

Bitter lawsuits followed. American revoked Steven's pass and he sued for breach of contract. They sued him back. Many years later and hundreds of thousands of dollars in legal fees led to American Airlines and Steven Rothstein coming to an out-of-court settlement, although the full details are not allowed to be disclosed by any party.

The data lied. And real consequences were felt, not only in dollars lost but in livelihoods lost. Steven was proud of his pass and traveling became part of his identity, and American Airlines staff became like an extended family. Yet all that ended. Even worse, there were more lawsuits. More people out there[14] like Steven are currently in litigation over the issue.[15] All could have been avoided by using my superpower #9 to Question the Data and really understand the metrics.

Questioning the metrics to unearth what their actual meaning is may be one of the most important things you can do in your business and career, and doing so these days has never been more important. It seems as if social media happens to take up a mythological level of truth in our society, and addiction to clicks, views, and "likes" take on meaning far beyond validity. We somehow view social media as truth. How did it get this way? And what can we learn about Questioning the Data from looking at social media? Take a look below for tool #1 which questions the data and helps us understand the real meaning of the social media metrics.

Tool #1: You Need More Than Likes: The Gut Check

It seems that the metrics on social media are straightforward. The more views, likes, and clicks, the more a person or product is popular or validated. That is pretty much it in the social media world. But what exactly does that mean? If someone clicks, does it mean they are engaged? Does it mean they are interested? Did they click by mistake? Did they buy something?

My research into Questioning the Data has led to me to see that social media is rife with so called "vanity metrics."[16] What vanity metrics track is a data set that is inherently not useful. Things like clicks or likes or traffic. On their own the data may provide some limited use, but overall the usefulness of this data set is low. They are called "vanity metrics" because they produce a feel-good measurement that does not reflect an actual value. In other words, the data may look impressive at first but is not a true indicator of something you can take action on.

You may get a lot of likes on a recent post. Great. Now what? You may get a few views (or many views) on your website. Amazing. Now what? You may get a ton of clicks. Fantastic. Now what?

Actionable metrics as opposed to vanity metrics are decision point metrics that allow you to take some sort of action that will move you forward. They answer the "so what?" question by providing you a path forward. The "so what" question may be a business decision that you can make from the metrics, it may be a replication attempt of the results to make sure it's not a fluke, or it can be zeroing in on one result and checking to see if it provides actionable value. But at the end of the day, it's all a hollow and vain approach unless you use my first tool in the Question the Data superpower, which is to conduct a gut check.

A gut check will allow you to test the data and metrics to see if they actually make sense. Sure you applied all the tools from earlier in the chapter, but the one thing we have not covered is the self-questioning that a gut check can provide, which is essential. It's a moment of reflection that will give you some well-deserved insight. It is the truth that gives you action that makes sense for you. What may be universally true for someone else rings false or phony for you. What seems like a no brainer for someone else may be a hard no for you. Thinking beyond the data and meshing it with a gut check is a true way to make your actions authentic. Here are some amazing case studies where a gut check overcame the data:

- The band Rush was told to dress more hip by their record label. That's what the data showed, that kids like bands that were dressed more hip. They were told to change their music style to be more contemporary and shorten the length of their songs to be Top 40 radio friendly. That's what the data showed as a path to success. They did none of this[17] yet achieved worldwide renown and are now members of the Rock and Roll Hall of Fame. They became legendary in the Rock and Roll world by trusting their gut and never losing sight as to what made them authentic as a band. When the data came in, they did a gut check. No matter what the data may have shown, a simple gut check was an override that led to success.

- Frederick Smith's FedEx overnight delivery business model was called impossible by most analysts because the data showed that it wouldn't work. The data showed that there were just too many things that could go wrong, and the coordination between an airplane and a truck to take a package to its final destination was risky and fraught with data that showed potential failure points.[18] After operating at a loss for more than two years, FedEx was profitable and broke the mold of the delivery business. Frederick did this by trusting his gut that it could be possible. Not the data. He knew instinctively because he was a pilot[19] that he could get a plane in and out of a location fast – so he trusted his pilot's gut and went against all the naysayers to launch one of the most successful companies in US history. Today FedEx is recognized as one of the most successful companies in the world.[20]

- Steve Ellis saw the data. And it was ugly. It showed that fast food was just that: fast food. That no one would pay extra for fast food that was served with integrity[21]: integrity of quality ingredients and in preparation. Data set after data set showed that this would fail as "conventional wisdom" deduced from the data held that the fast food business is simply a race to the bottom – about finding efficiencies above all else and that a cash strapped consumer wouldn't pay a dime more than necessary. Get the food cheaper above all. But Steve's gut told him something different. His gut told him that indeed people would be willing to pay a bit more for fast food if it was made well, fresh, and tasted great. And so he launched his fast food restaurant Chipotle on high-quality fresh ingredients, sustainable farming techniques, and an open-kitchen concept where people can see their food being prepared. Today Chipotle is one of the most successful fast-causal concepts, having revolutionized fast-casual dining.[22] All this success came at odds with the data.

Perhaps you can be the next visionary who leads by trusting your gut and launching into something that you know will authentically connect with a given audience to make your venture – be it career or business – successful as well. When we Question the Data and trust our gut we can make decisions that have a profound effect on our success without taking the data at face value and blindly following whatever it says.

Tool #2: Beware the Demagogues

The demagogue is a person or persons who spew out at the highest possible volume their particular opinion of something. And in reality they are everywhere. On college campuses, in our boardrooms, on social channels, and in our media. And they can be aggressive, making it hard for us to hear our own thoughts sometimes. We need creativity to avoid simply following what everyone else is doing – even if it is coming from the loudest source possible. We need to come up with the right questions, do some detective work, and educate ourselves on the classics in order to drown out all the shouting to make decisions on our own. It is not productive to take their so-called "information" on faith. Especially when it is shouted out by the loudest voice.

Unfortunately, if you look carefully enough you will find that many people are often susceptible to the range of things they hear – especially from the demogogues whose sole purpose is not the propagation of truth, it's the propagation of themselves.

Demagogues have propagated fake and quite frankly disruptive theories, and they can be found all over the internet. The thing is that they cause very real damage – their opinions distort the very fabric of history just to earn a few clicks, a few likes, and some attention.

The demagogue can also appear in the workplace. In this case they are the loudest person in the room always first to answer and first to know everything. They are the person that will get behind anything they deem valuable for their career or their personal path, not the vision of the company or organization. We all can most likely name a few of these people that we have encountered over our careers. They are everywhere. And that's why it's so important to recognize the demagogue and not fall under their spell. It may be hard to go against the prevailing wind. It may be hard to counter the demagogue's narrative. But it's imperative if we ever hope to find the truth and build wisdom into our decision making.

Tool #3: Seek Balance

On one hand, seeking metrics and something that can be reflected by a number is often comforting. We feel as if numbers represent something "real" and tangible. We love our spreadsheets, charts, graphs, and numbers. They give us a feeling of control. If we can measure something then we feel as if we understand it. We feel that everyone is using metrics of some sort to measure something. And we don't want to be left out. Metrics and data and analytics are the cornerstone of measuring success that we so badly want. And it is that success that we are all after.

On the other hand, creativity and innovation tell us that the numbers don't matter. That the numbers are deceiving. They are misleading because what we choose to measure is often things that are easily measurable. Like distance or sales numbers. But creativity and innovation tell us that the most important metrics are unmeasurable: The desirability of a new product or the joy it brings someone. Creativity and innovation show us that the soft skills at work cannot be measured either. Skills like empathy or humor or integrity or joy.

The best things in life cannot be measured or quantified either. How can we measure the love of a child, the beauty of a color, the exquisite taste of a proper key lime pie, the amazingness of our friendships, the connectivity and rapport we have with that client that far transcends work? These are some of the most important things in life, so why are we trying to quantify that?

The secret to using analytics and creativity is to balance the two. Balance is the secret. All the numbers, quantification, estimates, and KPIs in the world will not make sense if your strategy is not first and foremost creative. Then the numbers will make sense. That creativity strategy will give you the judgment you need to make a call on the data that you receive. Without the creativity and innovation as a method to digest the data you have received to make a judgment on it, your decision making is flawed and is half as good as it could be if it instead were fully balanced.

It is like making a decision with half the information.

We would never willingly make a decision with half the facts, yet we do it at work everyday when we ignore the gut check, the creative approach, and the myriad other soft skill decision points that will lead us to a more balanced and nuanced place. Here are some ways to balance creativity with data to reach a harmonious outlook at work and beyond work:

1. **Context Is Everything**. Imagine if I told you that a particular stock just went down 12% today. That would be pretty bad, right? But without any context, that news means close to nothing. Because the greater context would show that since you purchased the stock it has gained 40%, and the 12% dip

still has you up by 28%. It's all about the context in buying
and trading securities, and it is the same with establishing
metrics and data as the baseline of your career or business.

Let's say you are in the market for some new software
to take care of a pesky issue at work. You have the choice
of three different software companies – and all of them do
more or less the same thing. One of them is feature packed,
which makes it attractive as you can use it to solve a whole
host of issues; another is less feature packed; and finally the
third has one or two features you expect from the software
and they work really well. Most people would choose the
feature rich software because they think they are getting the
most bang for their buck. How could you not! On paper
the feature rich software makes sense. That's what the data
shows. But when you add creative thinking to the mix, you
begin to ask relevant questions. Questions like who's going
to use the software? Is it going to require additional training? What do I really need this thing to do well after all?
And finally, you may come to the conclusion that the software that offers the fewest options but does the one or two
tasks really well may be the best bet. Because people can
start to use it right away, instead of complaining about having to learn something new.

Context matters to a data or analytic source. Because
while the numbers can be theoretical, life is not lived in theory. It is lived in the real world where the adoption of this new
software, for example, may be the biggest challenge. People
will reject using it on some of the most archaic reasons such
as they don't like the color of it or they think it takes too long
to configure. Context of the data is everything. And applying
a real world filter into the data set can mean the difference
between widespread adoption and outright rejection.

2. **Reality Is Complex.** What may look good on paper – the metrics say it will look good – may not play out that way in real life. Without balancing the metrics with how they may appear in real life, we are left without a chance our idea will do well. Real life is super complex and features many factors that affect the success of a venture. Take for example the story about American Airlines and their AAirpass from earlier in the chapter. What looked good on paper did not exactly pan out that way in reality. Or look at the Segway personal mobility device that was supposed to change the world.[23] The metrics had shown that it would revolutionize personal mobility. But in the real world it was dang awkward! Users looked kind of silly riding on it, and it quickly vanished into the annals of history. The metrics may have shown a revolution, but in real life it made people look silly and awkward as they rode them. And pop culture soon made them the butt of late-night comedic routines and jokes.[24]

   Reality is complex at the end of the day, with something as arbitrary as how someone looks while they use a product being a deciding factor on ruining the revolution of personal mobility. While data and metrics are important, they aren't enough on their own. Without the creativity to assess the complexity of reality, an idea that looks good on paper may fail to gain traction in real life.

3. **Balance Metrics and Non-metric Perspectives.** Metrics and the pursuit of data need to be moderated with judgment. That judgment will come to us only if we think with a Solution Mindset, one embedded with creativity and innovation. Once we have a set of data, and we make a judgment on its appropriateness to act or not act upon the data, we must now find the balance in order to appraise its value. For example, charts and graphs may help us detect some

useful data, but we now infuse that data with other sources of non-quantifiable, non-metric perspectives: communication, Questioning the Data, meetings with stakeholders, meetings with the consumers, seeing if something is perceived to be "cool" or not, and other methods that may not be quantifiable yet hold immense value. Then we combine the necessary data with the non-quantifiable "data" and we can make a decision that has a far better chance of passing the "real world" test.

For example, Segway found that people didn't want to look like dorks on their scooters, so maybe a different design could have prevented that? Not looking like a dork is different to everyone, yet Segway may have found some balance in the look and feel of the scooter to make it more palatable from a non-quantifiable perspective. When we look to balance the metrics with non-metric perspectives, we allow real-world unquantifiable information to affect our product or service or even career. And that may be one of the biggest deciding factors between a successful path and one that fails.

Not all numbers are bad. It's how we use them. And deciding to use the numbers in a way that gives us the most benefit for real-world success is everything. In a world that seeks to quantify every last bit, having the perspective to assess value from quantification yet balance it with what is happening in the real world will make a superpower out of Questioning the Data.

Conclusion

In this chapter we learned about the ninth superpower and all the ways we need to Question the Data to give us creative and innovative superpowers. We looked at the man who flew too much, metrics that didn't reflect reality, and the myth of overpopulation. Now we will explore superpower #10, which features perhaps the toughest challenge yet: What the things we tell ourselves teach us about our own unique problem-solving superpowers. Sometimes to be the most creative and innovative person, you must look at who you are as a person first. It may surprise you to learn that everyone is born creative, and finding that inner ability to solve any problem may be the ticket to embracing your Solution Mindset.

Superpower #10: There's No Comparison

What the Things We Tell Ourselves Teach Us About Our Own Unique Problem-Solving Superpowers

When I enter most intimately into what I call myself I always stumble on some particular perception or other and never can observe anything but the perception.

—David Hume

Therapists will tell you that we are so dang unhappy all the time[1] because we continually compare ourselves to others. Your neighbor has a greener lawn and a cooler car. Your friend from the PTA's kid gets better grades. Your high school buddy has such an impressive career. And your coworker gets paid so much more for doing the same job.

189

Scientists have a name for this type of comparison that we do – they call it Social Comparison Theory. It was founded by Leon Festinger in 1954 in a seminal study[2] where he coined the term Social Comparison Theory with the idea that humans have to gain some sort of accurate self-evaluation based on seeing how we compare to others. In other words, it's a check that we conduct to see how we stack up to others around us on things like wealth, attractiveness, sophistication, intelligence, and success.

Leon's study came out in the 1950s when there was a lot to compare yourself to others on. Things like who had the greener grass or made more money for doing the same job or who's kids seemed better behaved than yours. But the 1950s were limited in the scope of media – usually comparing yourself to others stayed local: your neighborhood, your school, or your workplace. Or maybe what you saw on the four TV stations[3] that were broadcast to your area.

Over 70 years have passed since the initial study was completed. Today, the immediacy of the internet and apps take comparing yourself to others to a whole new level.

A ton of major studies show how damaging and problematic social media can be with academic sounding titles like "Social comparisons: A potential mechanism linking problematic social media use with depression"[4] and "Associations between social media use and depression among US young adults"[5] and who can forget "Problematic social networking site use and comorbid psychiatric disorders: A systematic review of recent large-scale studies."[6] What all these studies[7] and others[8] have found is simple: social media is bad for you. Pretty much that's it. It's a wonder that people use social media at all.

Think about it: when was the last time you used social media and had a positive interaction – much less felt better after using it? Can't remember? Perhaps the answer is even "never." I can't recall a single time after using Facebook or LinkedIn or Twitter (now X) or Instagram or any of the other social media apps that left me feeling better about myself. In fact, the opposite is true. As most of these studies have shown, the incessant nature of social media is a unique way of drawing us in and making us compare ourselves to others. It is especially problematic when social media seems to show people in their most positive light and seldom what you see online is an accurate representation of someone's life.[9]

It's easy to spiral: everyone seems smarter, richer, happier, and, well, so much better than you. And this ruins our ability to approach and solve problems creatively.

But there's hope. Every single human being on Earth is born with an indomitable spirit of creativity that has been given to you by your maker. It is truly one of the most fantastic gifts of life. And that is the gift of creativity. Found in the pages of this book is a recipe for using that gift to better your lot. No matter what it is that you want to do. This last chapter highlights my unique superpower #10, which simply states that There's No Comparison.

When we compare ourselves to others, we are never really comparing apples to apples. Because no two people are the same, so therefore no two applications of The Solution Mindset are the same. All that time we spend comparing ourselves to others is a waste. Creativity is deeply held within every human being. And the way that you practice creativity is not the way that anyone else will practice creativity. So, when social media forces us to compare our perception of our accomplishments, prestige, and success to those of others, it's a moot point. Why? Because it's all smoke and mirrors. And not truth. Creativity is the main differentiator between all humans, and therefore there really is no comparison between you and anyone else.

In fact, it's in our DNA. Scientists have recently identified 267 genes unique to human DNA that drive our creativity, including "innovativeness, flexibility, depth of planning, and related cognitive abilities for symbolism and self-awareness that also enable spontaneous generation of narrative art and language."[10] That literally means that creativity is in our DNA – it is what differentiates us from other animals and other humans, too. The role that these particular 267 genes play in our lives is the gift that our ancestors have given to us from the past: it's the gift of continued survival.

There is no survival on Earth possible for humans without creativity. It is what got humans where we are today. The innovation of a cave as shelter has turned into the houses we live in today. The innovation of fire has led us to the air-conditioned and heated world we live in today. The domestication of the horse has taken us into rockets that reach the heavens and will soon take us to the planet Mars. These genes are the central component of humanity that has allowed us to soar, to accomplish, to master our environments.

There is no problem on Earth that is beyond repair. There is no challenge that is too difficult to surmount. There is no mountain too high to climb. Human ingenuity is the differentiator – and there is nothing out of reach that creativity, innovation, and a Solution Mindset cannot cure. From the smallest issue to the largest, as individuals, we all have different combinations of creative traits that are exclusive to us because of our own unique DNA.

Some of you reading may want to solve issues at the workplace that seem insurmountable. Some of you may want to change your community or the world that we live in. And in each case, The Solution Mindset is a view that sees no challenge beyond the pale of resolution. No issue is beyond fixing. From solving the riddle of disease to establishing sustainable systems at work, the common denominator in both tasks – which seems wildly different at first glance – is that both require a Solution

Mindset to achieve. While the path to solve each task is completely different, they are held together by the connected thread of innovation and creativity.

The Bottom Line on Creativity

Some of the greatest value we can bring to our workplace in the twenty-first century emanates from our ability to apply creative and innovative problem-solving techniques. The effect of creativity on the bottom line is significant and has been proven in several different studies. Let's take a quick look at three different studies related to this. The first is purely academic, the second is a mix of academic and real-world findings, and the third is purely based on real-world findings. These studies and more should once and for all settle the debate on creativity in the workplace and its effect on improvements not only on the bottom line, but in many other beneficial ways too:

- On the purely academic front, a study completed in late 2023 by Michelle Leanne Oppert and her team has shown that despite many years of study, debate, research, and empirical results, the value of creativity has remained elusive. So she and her team set out to see if they can qualify the value of creativity. Her team has found that creativity is "predominantly instrumental" in the application of "achieving outcomes"[11] no matter what it was applied to.

- A mixed academic/real-world study by the World Economic Forum on the future of jobs found that 73% of employers surveyed reported that creative thinking skills were a top priority when considering talent as we move into the future.[12]

- A recent real-world study conducted by Harvard Business Review Analytics Services and Canva[13] found 96%

of those surveyed agree that creative ideas are essential to long-term success and that 94% of professionals surveyed believed that organizations that invest in creativity and innovation will be more successful than others in the twenty-first century.

The bottom line is that the more creativity and innovation are studied, the more they reveal how effective their problem-solving powers are. When we use superpower #10, our individuality in using our own creative and innovative thoughts and plans become our very DNA – our sole identity in solving issues that were once unsolvable.

Creative thinking is also an exclusively human skill that no artificial intelligence can replace. The originality of ideas that are generated by human beings – especially within the confines of *The Solution Mindset* and the 10 superpowers found in these pages – differentiates human beings from the latest innovations in machine learning and AI. Both can seem impressive at first, but they are no replacement for human ingenuity. Humans can outperform AI in even the most rigorous tests[14] and will continue to do so forever. There is no machine, however advanced, that can ever replace human ingenuity. It is no wonder that all these studies repeatedly find that creativity, innovation, and the power humans have to solve problems are always a skill in demand, because there is nothing else that can solve problems quite the same way as human beings. All this discussion about humans beings and our ability to outshine even the most complex machines and computers got me thinking quite a lot about the Olympics.

Tool #1: A Positive Spin

I love the Olympics. They happen every two years and are one of those rare events that bring the world together to compete in sports. There is always the underdog story of the person who comes out of nowhere to unexpectedly win the Gold, there is always the story of the athlete who missed the cut and took over at the last second after someone got injured, and the little followed sport in which a small group of people retain fierce rivalries for esoteric reasons rife with superstition. Yep, I love the Olympics.

One of the best things about the Olympics is that they are an inherently human experience. It is basically humans competing with each other to see who can run faster by a fraction of a second. And the innovations seen on the field come in slow progressions over many years, because except for the occasional cheating or doping scandal, human achievement at the Olympics is measured by fractions of a second over time.

Take for instance the men's 100-meter dash. The 100-meter dash is one of the most prestigious races in all of the Olympics in the Track and Field segment. If you are perhaps unfamiliar with it, its genius is in its simplicity: Several runners line up on the same line and have to run 100 meters to the finish line. That's it. Whomever gets to the finish line first wins Gold, second wins Silver, and the third place gets Bronze.

The first 100-meter race to be ratified by officials occurred in 1912,[15] even though the event has been run since 1896. The 100-meter dash in the 1912 Olympics was won by Ralph Craig[16] of the United States with a time of 10.8 seconds – which even by today's standards is extraordinarily quick. Contrast that with the modern world record held today by Usain Bolt, which is 9.58 seconds accomplished in 2009. From the time records were kept all the way up until today, the improvement in 100-meter race times in over 110 years has been 1.22 seconds.[17] From Ralph Craig to Usain Bolt, all that separates them is 1.22 seconds. About the time it takes you to read the word: *time*.

Now, there are many ways to look at this. At first glance it may be disappointing to see that in over a hundred years improvements have been so slight. You may look at this as a failure of real and tangible results. And perhaps that is the view that most people would take. But in using this tool #1 A Positive Spin, we learn how to put A Positive Spin on results and look deep within the improvements to recognize extraordinary growth. And while 1.22 seconds may not seem like a long time to you or me, in the running world, it is an eternity.

The 1.22 seconds of improvement is quite extraordinary. When we use A Positive Spin to look at data or performance reviews at work or anything that can be measured, we will be able to see things as an actual improvement that many others may miss. And what seems like a slight improvement may actually be worthwhile and noteworthy. Take for instance this 100-meter dash race: There have been significant improvements over the years. Shoe technology has improved and made grip better. Timing technology has improved as well as training, technique, and diet. All these improvements have been significant to the 100-meter dash and have resulted in momentous improvements in race times. Often times a 100-meter dash race will be decided by a tenth of a second. Race results from Usain Bolt's world record race of 9.58 seconds show competitor Darvis Patton coming in at last place at 10.34 seconds in the same race, making the difference between first and last place less than a second.[18] It's all how you look at it – and we can choose to look at it with A Positive Spin. Darvis Patton with 10.43 seconds would have been an Olympic champion had he run the race in 1912.

So, is there a difference in first- and second-place finishers at the Olympics? Or even in first-, second-, and third-place finishers? I set out to see what the difference was, and the results are extraordinary.

A research study on Olympic athletes revealed some unexpected results about our ability to see situations differently.[19] You would think that first-place, second-place, and third-place finishers were equally happy, right? Wrong.

Surprisingly, Bronze medal winners were much happier than those who won Silver. Bronze winners felt that they were just happy to be on the medal stand, while second-place finishers were disappointed more about losing out to first place than they were about finishing second. Silver winners saw themselves as having come so close to Gold and then missing out, whereas Bronze winners felt elated that they beat out those in fourth, fifth, and sixth places to make it to the top three. There are many ways to look at any problem. It is your choice to look at it in a positive way. A positive mind doesn't shut down new ideas but instead enables you to approach situations with A Positive Spin.

Tool #2: You as No One Else

Now that we have established that creativity is unique to every person on earth, we can use tool #2 You as No One Else to unveil what it is that makes you unique. Now it is time to uncover what it is that makes you so irreplaceable and your problem-solving skills matchless anywhere in the world.

When we compare ourselves to others, we cheat ourselves out of the opportunity to express the very superpower our own DNA gives us: the power of individualized creativity as realized by the one and only YOU.

That's why some of us are more creative at visual arts while others find creativity through problem solving (for example, those scientists who discovered 267 genes in DNA exhibited unbelievable creative problem-solving skills). For some, creativity comes in finding new ways to make mundane work fun, while for others it's using creative language to help bring together people who can't agree. Perhaps your expression of creativity will be different, or:

- Perhaps your expression of creativity will be something like Kim Perell, an entrepreneur that started her career with nothing. Kim started her marketing company with $10,000 and plenty of credit card debt after her first company went bankrupt during the tech bubble. So what exactly did she do? She came up with a plan at her in-laws' kitchen table to launch her own marketing firm.[20] She saw that she had 10k, a bunch of credit card debt, and said – you know what – let's go for it. Kim's particular tool #2 You as No One Else is that she didn't let her failures define her and she corrected her mistakes by starting her second company. For her in particular, a focus on execution was the key differentiator between failure and success. She handled the execution as only she could do, her and no one else.

- Perhaps your expression of creativity will be something like designer Vera Wang. She started her business at age 40 because she was having a tough time as an "older bride" finding the wedding dress of her dreams. Her specific implementation of tool #2 You as No One Else gave her a unique perspective on the market of bridal stores. She made the calculated risk of taking her previous experience in the fashion industry and starting her own brand because she was certain that she could introduce something new and different into the bridal industry.[21] She did things like no one else. For her in particular, she felt passionate about hard, unending, grinding work. And so she applied her skills in a way that no one else could do and launched a multimillion dollar fashion brand that has since expanded to eyewear, fragrance, jewelry, and more.

- Perhaps your expression of creativity will be something like Or Offer. He started his company after years of working in his parents' jewelry business. His parents kept telling him there was no money in custom jewelry, and he had felt the feast and famine patterns throughout his childhood when times were good and times were lean. So by helping his parents in their business, he discovered that it was next to impossible to find similar jewelry designers to what his parents were doing,[22] and so his company was born, Similar-Web, which today is a $1.8 billon dollar company of which he is the CEO and founder. Or did things like no one else. For him in particular, he wanted to quit the business literally 10 times over the years but forced himself to stay in. So he applied his perseverance in a way that no one else can do. Getting to the finish line was Or's unique use of tool #2 You as No One Else.

Now it's your turn. You are as no one else who ever existed and will in the future exist on earth. And your gifts of creativity and innovation have hopefully been enhanced with the passage of the chapters of this book. Ask yourself the following questions to get started:

1. **What Am I Really Good At?** Is there something that comes easy to you and that you can execute without any effort? Perhaps you are a wiz at Excel or maybe you're effortless at meeting people – strangers – and talking to them. Find what it is that comes naturally to you that you may excel at.

This should be something that you don't even think about as a skill. It is just who you are.

2. **What Do Others Think I'm Good At?** Have you ever had a boss, or perhaps several friends have told you that you are really good at a particular thing? Maybe it's empathy and that you are great at making people feel heard. Or maybe you are a tinkerer and are great at tearing apart things to build them back up again better than before. Again, these skills are unique to who you are and are applications of the #2 tool in the There's No Comparison superpower.

3. **What Do I Really Want to Do?** Perhaps you want to surf all day or perhaps you want to work and grind it out. Every person is different and finding your passion and what drives you can be an exhilarating experience. Once you have identified a few of those traits, you can then apply them to what makes you truly unique in the world. Because even if you like surfing, there is likely some unique thing that fascinates you about the sport. And likewise, if you enjoy the grind, there is an aspect or satisfaction that you derive from hard work that others may not be able to clearly see.

You as No One Else is one of the most important tools you can use in the quest to create a Solution Mindset. As we have seen with the stories of some of the greatest minds in modern business from Or Offer to Vera Wang, recognizing and nurturing your unique gift enables you to solve issues in a way that no one else can solve them.

Tool #3: Make Something from Nothing

As we round out this last tool under the There's No Comparison superpower, we have to take some time to look at the concept of making something out of nothing. Because at the end of the day, that is what creativity is all about.

Your ability to take your world and make from it something new is nothing short of extraordinary. At work. At home. And beyond.

Why is that so extraordinary? Why is creativity and innovation Making Something from Nothing so powerful?

The ancient philosopher Cicero believed that unity and cognition expressed in language, painting, art, sculpture, poetry, public speaking, or music provide a philosophical justification for any creative endeavor.[23] In other words, Cicero believed that the expression of creativity, as long as it was unified and cognitive, was a worthwhile human expression. It's pretty much a Solution Mindset that he is speaking of – one that is well organized (Cicero calls this "unity") and one that makes sense for a particular use case (Cicero calls this "cognitive") which is what this book is full of.

Yet Cicero takes it a bit further, and this is where it starts to get good. Cicero believed that to speak or write or paint well, expressions of creativity serve to reignite the spark of divinity held deep within us. That expressing creativity makes us closer to a divine spirit. He goes on to say that creative expression also helps us align ourselves with the movement of the cosmos. In other words, to the Ancient Greeks, the movement of the cosmos was pretty much an expression of living in accordance to nature or "closer to nature" or a "natural state" humans could find themselves in as they practiced creativity. For Cicero, creativity was a natural part of being human – an idea he articulated centuries before modern science demonstrated that creativity is encoded in our DNA. Isn't that incredible?

According to the ancients, choosing creativity – whether in the classical sense of painting or sculpture, or in the modern sense of solving problems at work and beyond – was a way for humans to move closer to divinity, to a more perfect state of being. They saw it as a choice: to embrace creativity in all that we do. Cicero believed that creativity ultimately guided human beings toward something higher, bringing us ever closer to the truth.

The pursuit of truth is ultimately the grand culmination of our creative spirit. Our collective innovative soul leads us to tool #3. This relies on inherently creative attributes, some of which are listed below:

1. **Stay Curious.** If you are fascinated by the world around you, you are seeking truth without even trying. Staying continually interested by asking questions, seeking meaning, and being inspired by solutions you see every day will keep you on a path of the pursuit of truth. There is nothing that darkness fears more than light, so by continually being curious you are brandishing light into dark corners, forever exploring the world by staying curious.

2. **Appreciate Nuance.** Not all information is to be taken at face value. Sometimes that information features sarcasm or subtext or some other lawyer that only the informed would understand. Appreciating nuance even in a meeting at work will help you seek truth and understand that it may come in different forms from what you expect.

3. **Maintain Integrity.** Keep healthy stock of what it is that you value. It can be charity, it can be enterprise, it can be generosity or gentleness. No matter what DNA makes you a creative and innovative person, your value system will be different from anyone else's. Perhaps integrity to you looks like Chuck Feeney.[24] The billionaire founder of the Duty Free Shops we all know and love gave away, anonymously, his entire fortune of at least $8 billion dollars. Yep, even his kids didn't inherit a dime. Integrity is what you value.

4. **Cultivate Open-Mindedness.** Having an open mind to see, evaluate, and change your perspective is critical. Having the ability to shift your perspective as new information comes in is essential to finding the truth. Holding on to beliefs too rigidly clouds your evolution into a truth-seeking human being.

5. **Pursue Beauty.** If we learned anything from the Ancient Greeks of Athens who founded our way of thinking and from Jerusalem where the moral heart of Western humanity originated from, we learned that the pursuit of beauty is not vanity. What it is instead is a pursuit of harmony, symmetry, and proportion. In the ancient teachings, beauty is synonymous with goodness. In Plato's symposium,[25] beauty and the pursuit of it become a form of ultimate knowledge. Look for beauty in everyday objects, people, and see a world of harmony, symmetry, and order. Albert Einstein once said,[26] *"Study and the pursuit of truth and beauty is a sphere of activity in which we are permitted to remain children all our lives."*

6. **Develop Grit.** Teddy Roosevelt remarked during a speech[27] in 1899 that, *"It is hard to fail, but it is worse never to have tried to succeed. In this life we get nothing save by effort."* Later in an address[28] in 1910 he said, *"I have never in my life envied a human being who led an easy life; I have envied a great many people who led difficult lives and led them well."* The development of grit and our ability to remain resilient is one of the most important creative and innovative skills we have. And the development and maintenance of grit in our everyday lives will serve us well to overcome any challenge.

7. **Have Patience.** Having the ability to play the long game takes patience. Also, knowing that not every issue can (nor should) be solved right this second takes patience. Patience is a virtue that understands that sometimes a Solution Mindset can take years to yield fruit and that the best thing you can

do is nothing. Stick to long game and allow your investments to provide growth over time.

Making Something from Nothing relies on some of the above seven creative attributes that have a substantial impact on your creative and innovate future. So, when I say that your ability to take your world and make from it something new and different is nothing short of extraordinary, you can now look at it in the context of being both closer to divinity and closer to the truth. And that goes for anything you apply your newfound creativity to.

Maybe it's your ability to create something from scratch as someone who can take raw elements and make something new from it. Or maybe it's to modify something existing as someone who can take what exists and add to it something novel or unique. Or even putting together several different things into one streamlined idea as someone who can put together several different creative initiatives into a single use case.

All these implementations of creativity have one common denominator: the way that you express your creativity is valid and quite frankly urgently needed in a world that is changing rapidly.

Conclusion

In this chapter we learned about the tenth and final superpower and all the ways that there is "no comparison" between you and anyone else. We saw how social media makes us unhappy, how creativity is in our DNA, and how creativity can be a financially beneficial entity.

Now, the book is coming to an end, but that doesn't have to be the end of our journey together. Find me online at nirbashan.com and keep me in the loop with how you are progressing. I cherish emails from around the world, and while

I cannot get back to every reader, I will do as much as I can to keep supporting you in any way that I can.

You are now faced with a choice – a call to action, a galvanizing leap forward. The past belongs to others, but the future rests with you. My hope is that you choose a Solution Mindset in everything you do, and commit to bringing light into the world.

Because nothing is impossible with a Solution Mindset.

Notes

Introduction

1. KMTV 3 News Now Omaha. "KMTV 3 News Now Omaha," August 26, 2020. https://www.3newsnow.com/news/moving-forward/bellevue-police-officer-buys-car-seats-for-mom-in-need-during-traffic-stop.
2. Atrium Health. "Selfless Giving: Living Kidney Donors Like Laura Laxton Are Saving Lives," April 4, 2023. https://atriumhealth.org/dailydose/2023/04/04/laura-laxton-patient-story.
3. Rannard, Georgina. "Oceans Littered With 171 Trillion Plastic Pieces," BBC.com, March 8, 2023. https://www.bbc.com/news/science-environment-64889284.
4. The Ocean Cleanup. "The Ocean Cleanup," June 4, 2025. https://theoceancleanup.com/.
5. Searle, Julian. "Waste Management and Recycling | the Ocean Cleanup." The Ocean Cleanup, March 28, 2025. https://theoceancleanup.com/waste-management-and-recycling.
6. Hurford, Molly. "When This Bike Company Put a TV on Its Box, Shipping Damages Went Way Down." *Bicycling*, October 11, 2017. https://www.bicycling.com/news/a20027122/vanmoof-tv-on-box-damaged-bikes.

Chapter 1

1. National Youth Climate Activism Award. "Titouan Bernicot: Defender of the Reef," NationalYCAA.org, September 9, 2020. https://www.nationalycaa.org/inspiration-and-support/titouan-bernicot-defender-of-the-reef?.
2. Marsh, Ariana. "Marine Biologists Doubted Him. Now, He's Revolutionizing Coral Reef Restoration." *Harper's Bazaar*, October 24, 2023.

https://www.harpersbazaar.com/culture/a45585627/marine-biologists-doubted-him-now-hes-revolutionizing-coral-reef-restoration.

3. Tseng, Julie and Jordan Poppenk. "Brain Meta-state Transitions Demarcate Thoughts Across Task Contexts Exposing the Mental Noise of Trait Neuroticism," *Nature Communications* 11, no. 1 (2020). https://www.nature.com/articles/s41467-020-17255-9.

4. Hu, Charlotte. "Why Writing by Hand Is Better for Memory and Learning." *Scientific American*, July 30, 2024. https://www.scientificamer ican.com/article/why-writing-by-hand-is-better-for-memory-and-learning and Van Der Weel, F. R. and Audrey L. H. Van Der Meer. "Handwriting but Not Typewriting Leads to Widespread Brain Connectivity: A High-density EEG Study With Implications for the Classroom," *Frontiers in Psychology* 14 (2024). https://www.frontiersin.org/journals/psychology/articles/10.3389/fpsyg.2023.1219945/full.

5. Murphy, Mark. "Neuroscience Explains Why You Need to Write Down Your Goals if You Actually Want to Achieve Them." *Forbes*, April 15, 2018. https://www.forbes.com/sites/markmurphy/2018/04/15/neurosci ence-explains-why-you-need-to-write-down-your-goals-if-you-actually-want-to-achieve-them.

6. Gilbert, Sam J., Annika Boldt, Chhavi Sachdeva, Chiara Scarampi, and Pei-Chun Tsai. "Outsourcing Memory to External Tools: A Review of 'Intention Offloading'." *Psychonomic Bulletin & Review* 30, no. 1 (2022): 60–76. https://link.springer.com/article/10.3758/s13423-022-02139-4.

7. Lim, John. "A Man's Truck Fell off a Cliff and Into a River After He Followed Google Maps." *Mashable SEA | Latest Entertainment & Trending*, February 11, 2019. https://sea.mashable.com/tech/2251/a-mans-truck-fell-off-a-cliff-and-into-a-river-after-he-followed-google-maps.

8. Gray, Bradley E. "Avoiding Success: How Does Fear of Success Impact Today's Workforce?" CUNY Academic Works, September 2023. https://academicworks.cuny.edu/cgi/viewcontent.cgi?article=6625&con text=gc_etds.

9. van Dam, Nick, Jacqueline Brassey, and Arjen van Witteloostuijn. "Why You're Not Fulfilling Your Potential at Work." Association of MBAs, November 18, 2019. https://www.associationofmbas.info/why-youre-not-fulfilling-your-potential-at-work/.

10. Van Gelderen, Marco. "Using a comfort zone model and daily life situations to develop entrepreneurial competencies and an entrepreneurial mindset," *Frontiers in Psychology*, May 15, 2023. https://www.ncbi.nlm.nih.gov/pmc/articles/PMC10225726.

Chapter 2

1. Buffalo Trace Distillery. "Julian Van Winkle III Biography," n.d. https://www.buffalotracedistillery.com/media-kit/bios/julian-van-winkle-III.html?srsltid=AfmBOopM1Cz6RD8j2TRh4-2rBgI1gUq-etFRsLBZaeHfo76chSpq7xbM.
2. Buffalo Trace Distillery. "Pappy Van Winkle," n.d. https://www.buffalotracedistillery.com/legendary-people/van-winkle.html?srsltid=AfmBOorG3wsVMrerenklVEt63gSvUc4i73m_xsDZrqW1F-XrwtQS5PmJ.
3. Baumgartner, Thomas, Janek S. Lobmaier, Nicole Ruffieux, and Daria Knoch, "Feeling of guilt explains why people react differently to resource depletion warnings," Scientific Reports, June 7, 2021. https://pmc.ncbi.nlm.nih.gov/articles/PMC8185082/.
4. Nielsen, Rikke Sigmer, Christian Gamborg, and Thomas Bøker Lund. "Eco-guilt and Eco-shame in Everyday Life: An Exploratory Study of the Experiences, Triggers, and Reactions." *Frontiers in Sustainability* 5, 2024. https://www.frontiersin.org/journals/sustainability/articles/10.3389/frsus.2024.1357656/full.
5. Fernholz, Kathryn, Jim Bowyer, Gloria Erickson, Harry Groot, Mark Jacobs, Ashley McFarland, and Ed Pepke. "Forest Certification Update 2021: The Pace of Change." *Dovetail Partners.* Dovetail Partners, 2021. https://dovetailinc.org/upload/tmp/1611160123.pdf.
6. Szymkowski, Sean. "Michelin wants to replace oil with wood in tires," Motor Authority, July 22, 2018. https://www.motorauthority.com/news/1117646_michelin-wants-to-replace-oil-with-wood-in-tires.
7. McInerney, Ben. "How Many Trees Are Planted Each Year > Day > Minute." *GoTreeQuotes*, November 20, 2024. https://www.gotreequotes.com/how-many-trees-are-planted-each-year-month-day-minute-second/#:~:text=Approximately%201.9%20billion%20trees%20are,the%20United%20Nations%20Environmental%20program.
8. Chabad.org, "The Complete Jewish Bible with Rashi Commentary, Chapter 22," n.d. http://www.chabad.org/library/bible_cdo/16393/jewish/Chapter-22.htm.
9. Posner, Menachem. "The Ten Commandments," Chabad.org, n.d. https://www.chabad.org/library/article_cdo/aid/2896/jewish/What-Are-the-Ten-Commandments.htm#English.
10. The Scotsman, "Thou shalt not forget the Ten Commandments . . . except almost all of us have," June 4, 2009. https://www.scotsman.com/news/thou-shalt-not-forget-the-ten-commandments-except-almost-all-of-us-have-2479591.
11. Scott, John. "America Has a Retirement Crisis. We Need to Make It Easier to Save." *The Pew Charitable Trusts*, January 18, 2024. https://www.pewtrusts.org/en/about/news-room/opinion/2024/01/18/america-has-a-retirement-crisis-we-need-to-make-it-easier-to-save.

12. Lin, Judy T., Christopher Bumcrot, Tippy Ulicny, ARC Research, an SVC Company, Gary Mottola, Gerri Walsh, Robert Ganem, et al. "The State of U.S. Financial Capability: The 2018 National Financial Capability Study." *The State of U.S. Financial Capability: The 2018 National Financial Capability Study*, 2019. https://finrafoundation.org/sites/finrafoundation/ .files/NFCS-2018-Report-Natl-Findings.pdf.

13. Bearden, Bridget. "Retiree Reflections," *EBRI Issue Brief*, June 16, 2022. https://www.ebri.org/content/retiree-reflections.

14. Sekścińska, Katarzyna, Diana Jaworska, Joanna Rudzinska-Wojciechowska. "Self-Esteem and financial risk-taking," *Personality and Individual Differences* 172, April 2021. https://www.sciencedirect.com/ science/article/abs/pii/S0191886920307674.

15. BiaÅ, Aszek, Maciej Gaik Wojciech, Elton McGoun, and Piotr Zielonka. "Impulsive People Have a Compulsion for Immediate Gratification— Certain or Uncertain." *Frontiers in Psychology* 6 (2015). https:// pmc.ncbi.nlm.nih.gov/articles/PMC4419605/.

16. Microsoft. "Research Proves Your Brain Needs Breaks," April 20, 2021. https://www.microsoft.com/en-us/worklab/work-trend-index/brain-research.

17. Spataro, Jared. "The future of work–the good, the challenging & the unknown," Microsoft.com, July 8, 2020. https://www.microsoft.com/ en-us/microsoft-365/blog/2020/07/08/future-work-good-challenging-unknown/.

18. Ashforth, Blake E. "The experience of powerlessness in organizations," *Organizational Behavior and Human Decision Processes* 43(2), April 1989. https://www.sciencedirect.com/science/article/abs/pii/07495978 89900514.

Chapter 3

1. Meyers, Nechemia. "A straw that saves lives," *Cleveland Jewish News*, November 16, 2006. https://www.clevelandjewishnews.com/ archives/a-straw-that-saves-lives/article_18a158b0-73cf-5c80-878f-bb615a048f9f.html.

2. Shayo, Godfrey Michael, Elianaso Elimbinzi, Godlisten N. Shao, and Christina Fabian. "Severity of Waterborne Diseases in Developing Countries and the Effectiveness of Ceramic Filters for Improving Water Quality." *Bulletin of the National Research Centre/Bulletin of the National Research Center* 47, no. 1 (2023). https://bnrc.springeropen.com/articles/ 10.1186/s42269-023-01088-9.

3. Weizmann Institute of Science. "The Straw That Broke the Bacterium's Back," *Weizmann Wonder Wander*, August 25, 2016. https://wis-wander.weizmann.ac.il/earth-sciencesmade-institute/straw-broke-bacterium%E2%80%99s-back.

4. World Health Organization. "Cholera," Fact Sheet, December 5, 2024. https://www.who.int/news-room/fact-sheets/detail/cholera.

5. Water for Africa. "About Water for Africa," n.d. https://www.h2o4a.org/about.

6. Weizmann Institute of Science. "The Straw That Broke the Bacterium's Back," *Weizmann Wonder Wander*, August 25, 2016. https://wis-wander.weizmann.ac.il/earth-sciencesmade-institute/straw-broke-bacterium%E2%80%99s-back.

7. Konok, Veronika, Dóra Gigler, Boróka Mária Bereczky, and Ádám Miklósi. "Humans' attachment to their mobile phones and relationship with interpersonal attachment style," *Computers in Human Behavior* 61, August 2016. https://www.sciencedirect.com/science/article/abs/pii/S0747563216302333.

8. Wieland, Sören. "The Impact of Technological Distraction on Self-Actualization," Trinity College Dublin thesis, July 2018. https://www.researchgate.net/publication/369182918_THE_IMPACT_OF_TECHNOLOGICAL_DISTRACTION_ON_SELF-ACTUALIZATION.

9. Biskup, Martin J., Seth Kaplan, Jill C. Bradley-Geist, Ashley A. Membere. "Just how miserable is work? A meta-analysis comparing work and non-work affect," PLoS One 14(3), March 5, 2019. https://pmc.ncbi.nlm.nih.gov/articles/PMC6400410/.

10. Navarra, Katie. "Is the 'Great Regret' an Opportunity for a 'Great Return'?" SHRM.org, February 16, 2023. https://www.shrm.org/topics-tools/news/employee-relations/great-regret-opportunity-great-return.

11. Tomb, Devin. "72% of Muse Survey Respondents Say They've Experienced 'Shift Shock,'" The Muse, August 30, 2022. https://www.themuse.com/advice/shift-shock-muse-survey-2022.

12. CDC/National Center for Health Statistics. "Marriage and Divorce," Fast Stats, March 17, 2025. https://www.cdc.gov/nchs/fastats/marriage-divorce.htm.

13. Canales, Suany A. "Common reasons for divorce," The Open Respository at Binghamton University, January 31, 2021. https://orb.binghamton.edu/cgi/viewcontent.cgi?article=1020&context=hdev_fac.

14. Wilkinson & Finkbeiner. "Divorce Statistics: Over 115 Studies, Facts and Rates for 2024," n.d. https://www.wf-lawyers.com/divorce-statistics-and-facts/.

15. Leary, Mark R. "Emotional Responses to Interpersonal Rejection." *Dialogues in Clinical Neuroscience* 17, no. 4 (2015): 435–41. https://pmc.ncbi.nlm.nih.gov/articles/PMC4734881/.

16. Reynolds, Brady and Ryan M. Schiffbauer. "Impulsive choice and workplace safety: A new area of inquiry for research in occupational settings," *Behavioral Analysis* 27(2), Fall 2004. https://pmc.ncbi.nlm.nih.gov/articles/PMC2755405/.

17. Reynolds, Brady and Ryan M. Schiffbauer. "Impulsive choice and workplace safety: A new area of inquiry for research in occupational settings," *Behavioral Analysis* 27(2), Fall 2004. https://pmc.ncbi.nlm.nih.gov/articles/PMC2755405/.

18. American Psychological Association. "Multitasking: Switching costs," March 20, 2006. https://www.apa.org/topics/research/multitasking.

19. Duffy, Jill E. "How Much Time Do We Lose Task-Switching?" Productivity Report, April 11, 2025. https://productivityreport.org/2016/02/22/how-much-time-do-we-lose-task-switching/.

20. Pattison, Kermit. "Worker, Interrupted: The Costs of Task Switching," *Fast Company*, July 28, 2008. https://www.fastcompany.com/944128/worker-interrupted-cost-task-switching.

21. Bashan, Nir. "For Starters, It Keeps You Away From the Drama." *Psychology Today*, June 26, 2023. https://www.psychologytoday.com/us/blog/the-psychology-of-creativity/202306/why-you-should-not-make-friends-at-work.

22. Ellis, Lindsay. "Americans Are Breaking Up With Their Work Friends," *The Wall Street Journal*, August 17, 2022. https://www.wsj.com/articles/forget-work-friends-more-americans-are-all-business-on-the-job-11660736232.

23. Westfall, Brian. "Friends at Work? Today's Employees Aren't Interested," Capterra, March 3, 2022. https://www.capterra.com/resources/friends-at-work-research/.

Chapter 4

1. United Nations. "Young People's Potential, the Key to Africa's Sustainable Development," n.d. https://www.un.org/ohrlls/news/young-people's-potential-key-africa's-sustainable-development.

2. UNESCO UIS. "Education in Africa," December 2, 2019. https://uis.unesco.org/en/topic/education-africa.

3. UNESCO UIS. "263 Million Children and Youth Are Out of School," 27 April 2017. https://uis.unesco.org/en/news/263-million-children-and-youth-are-out-school.

4. Acmc, Edeh Samuel Chukwuemeka. "Countries With the Best Education System in Africa 2024: Top 17." *Bscholarly*, January 12, 2024. https://bscholarly.com/countries-with-the-best-education-system-in-africa/.

5. Acmc, Edeh Samuel Chukwuemeka, "Countries With the Best Education System in Africa 2024: Top 17," *Bscholarly*, January 12, 2024. https://bscholarly.com/countries-with-the-best-education-system-in-africa/# Ranking_of_the_Top_17_countries_with_the_best_education_system_ in_Africa_2024.

6. Trading Economics. "Seychelles - School Enrollment, Primary (% Gross) - 2025 Data 2026 Forecast 1970–2023 Historical," n.d. https://tradingeconomics.com/seychelles/school-enrollment-primary-percent-gross-wb-data.html#:~:text=Calendar,Temperature.

7. Seychelles Nation. "Seychelles' Education System Ranked First in Africa, 43rd in the World," n.d. https://www.nation.sc/articles/15130/seychelles-education-system-ranked-first-in-africa-43rd-in-the-world.

8. ADEA and Ministry of Education. "The Major Development Of Education In Seychelles [1977 to 1998]." Report. *Prospective Stock-Taking Review*, June 1999. https://www.adeanet.org/sites/default/files/pstr99_ seychelles.pdf.

9. Rusu, Marinela. "The Process of Self-Realization—From the Humanist Psychology Perspective," *Psychology* 10(8), June 2019. https://www.scirp.org/journal/paperinformation?paperid=93327.

10. Aksin-Sivrikaya, S. and C. B. Bhattacharya. "Where Digitalization Meets Sustainability: Opportunities and Challenges," In: Osburg, T., Lohrmann, C. (eds) Sustainability in a Digital World. CSR, Sustainability, Ethics & Governance. Springer, Cham. https://doi.org/10.1007/978-3-319-54603-2_3. See also: Schepers, S. (2017). "The Risk Averse Society: A Risk for Innovation?" In: Osburg, T., Lohrmann, C. (eds) *Sustainability in a Digital World. CSR, Sustainability, Ethics & Governance*. (Springer: 2017). https://doi.org/10.1007/978-3-319-54603-2_2.

11. Ryff, Carol D. "Self-realisation and Meaning Making in the Face of Adversity: A Eudaimonic Approach to Human Resilience." *Journal of Psychology in Africa* 24, no. 1 (2014): 1–12. https://pmc.ncbi.nlm.nih.gov/ articles/PMC4243302/.

12. Baumeister, Roy F. and Mark R. Leary. "The need to belong: Desire for interpersonal attachments as a fundamental human emotion," in *Interpersonal Development* (Routledge: 2007). https://www.taylorfrancis.com/ chapters/edit/10.4324/9781351153683-3/need-belong-desire-interper sonal-attachments-fundamental-human-motivation-roy-baumeister-mark-leary.

13. Martela, Frank, and Anne B. Pessi. "Significant Work Is About Self-Realization and Broader Purpose: Defining the Key Dimensions of

Meaningful Work." *Frontiers in Psychology* 9 (2018). https://www.frontier sin.org/journals/psychology/articles/10.3389/fpsyg.2018.00363/full.

14. American Psychiatric Association. "Rumination: A Cycle of Negative Thinking," Psychiatry.org, March 5, 2020. https://www.psychiatry.org/ news-room/apa-blogs/rumination-a-cycle-of-negative-thinking#:~:text= Rumination%20involves%20repetitive%20thinking%20or,then% 20contributes%20to%20more%20rumination.

15. Bennett, Hayley. "Why You Never Forget How to Ride a Bike, Explained by Neuroscience." *BBC Science Focus Magazine*, October 7, 2024. https://www.sciencefocus.com/science/why-do-we-never-forget-how-to-ride-a-bike.

16. Stiegler, Marjorie. "Why Do We Think the Grass Is Always Greener? Neuroscience," October 27, 2020. https://marjoriestieglermd.com/why-do-we-think-the-grass-is-always-greener-neuroscience/.

17. Segal, Gillian Zoe. "This Self-made Billionaire Failed the LSAT Twice, Then Sold Fax Machines for 7 Years Before Hitting Big—Here's How She Got There." CNBC, April 3, 2019. https://www.cnbc.com/2019/04/ 03/self-made-billionaire-spanx-founder-sara-blakely-sold-fax-machines-before-making-it-big.html?irclickid=yhB3f-Ss6xyPUuJQtrxBKXwx UkCV-LXlrU03Sk0&irgwc=1.

18. Karimi, Faith. "Behind the Staggering Success of Mr Beast," CNN.com, July 17, 2023. https://www.cnn.com/2023/07/15/entertainment/mrbeast-youtube-jimmy-donaldson-cec/index.html.

Chapter 5

1. Hart, Bradley W. "The Axis Powers of World War II," The National WWII Museum, August 28, 2024. https://www.nation alww2museum.org/war/articles/axis-powers-world-war-ii.

2. L. Stuart Hirai. "How the US and Japan Went From Enemies to Allies After WWII," History.com, n.d. https://www.history.com/news/post-wwii-us-japan-occupation-allies.

3. United States Institute of Peace. "A Guide to Understanding the History of the 'Comfort Women' Issue," University Writing Program, Brandeis University, April 30, 2022. https://www.usip.org/publications/ 2022/09/guide-understanding-history-comfort-women-issue.

4. Yang, Grace Danqing. "Cognitive Dissonance, Social Psychology, and Unit 731," University Writing Program, Brandeis University, April 30, 2022. https://www.brandeis.edu/writing-program/write-now/2022-2023/ yang-grace/index.html.

5. History.com Editors. "Bombing of Hiroshima and Nagasaki," History. com, July 18, 2025. https://www.history.com/topics/world-war-ii/bomb ing-of-hiroshima-and-nagasaki.

6. National Museum of the United States Army. "Douglas MacArthur," n.d. https://www.thenmusa.org/biographies/douglas-macarthur/.
7. Serafino, Nina, Curt Tarnoff, and Dick K. Nanto. "U.S. Occupation Assistance: Iraq, Germany and Japan Compared," CRS Report for Congress, March 23, 2006. https://www.history.navy.mil/research/library/online-reading-room/title-list-alphabetically/u/us-occupation-assistance-iraq-germany-japan-compared.html.
8. National Diet Library. "Reconstruction of Japan," n.d. https://www.ndl.go.jp/modern/e/cha5/index.html#:~:text=Japan%20accepted%20the%20terms%20of,policies%20of%20demilitarization%20and%20democratization.
9. Office of the Historian, "Milestones in the History of U.S. Foreign Relations: Occupation and Reconstruction of Japan, 1945–52," U.S. Department of State, n.d. https://history.state.gov/milestones/1945-1952/japan-reconstruction.
10. Kiey, Emma Donington. "State Shinto and Nationalism in Meiji Japan, by Emma Donington Kiey." The Manchester Historian, April 13, 2020. https://manchesterhistorian.com/2020/state-shinto-and-nationalism-in-meiji-japan-emma-donington.
11. Statista. "Ranking of Health and Health Systems of Countries Worldwide in 2023," September 24, 2024. https://www.statista.com/statistics/1376359/health-and-health-system-ranking-of-countries-worldwide/.
12. Katori, Teruyuki. "Japan's Healthcare Delivery System: From Its Historical Evolution to the Challenges of a Super-aged Society." *Global Health & Medicine* 6, no. 1 (2 February 2024): 6–12. https://pmc.ncbi.nlm.nih.gov/articles/PMC10912799/.
13. Wager, Emma. "What Drives Health Spending in the U.S. Compared to Other Countries?" Peterson-KFF Health System Tracker, August 2, 2024. https://www.healthsystemtracker.org/brief/what-drives-health-spending-in-the-u-s-compared-to-other-countries/.
14. Picchi, Aimee. "Americans Spend More on Health Care Than Any Other Nation. Yet Almost Half Can't Afford Care." *CBS News*, July 17, 2024. https://www.cbsnews.com/news/health-care-almost-half-of-americans-struggle-to-afford-medical-care/.
15. "About *JAMA*," JAMA Network, July 2025. https://jamanetwork.com/journals/jama/pages/for-authors.
16. Levitt, Larry, and Drew Altman. "Complexity in the US Health Care System Is the Enemy of Access and Affordability." *JAMA Health Forum* 4, no. 10 (2023): e234430. https://jamanetwork.com/journals/jama-health-forum/fullarticle/2811354.
17. Wagner, Emma, and Cynthia Cox. "International Comparison of Health Systems," KFF, October 2024. https://www.kff.org/health-policy-101-international-comparison-of-health-systems/.

18. WHO and Ministry of Health, Labour and Welfare, Japan. "Health Service Delivery Profile," 2012. https://citeseerx.ist.psu.edu/document? repid=rep1&type=pdf&doi=ebe5651c733c7e0d0f9024793041314671 00e519.

19. Japan Health Policy NOW. "Cost Control," n.d. https://japanhpn.org/ en/finan3/.

20. Kesh, Jonathan. "The Reason In-N-Out's Menu Has Hardly Changed," *Yahoo Life*, November 9, 2023. https://www.yahoo.com/lifestyle/reason-n-outs-menu-hardly-121530643.html.

21. Offer, Avner. "The American Automobile Frenzy of the 1950s," University of Oxford Discussion Papers in Economic and Social History, February 1997. https://www.researchgate.net/publication/5201270_ The_American_Automobile_Frenzy_of_the_1950s.

22. Ayling, Dominique. "The Incredible History of In-N-Out Burger," LoveFood.com, June 3, 2025. https://www.lovefood.com/gallerylist/ 166092/the-incredible-history-of-innout-burger.

23. Palmer, Karen. "How In-N-Out revolutionized the drive-thru in California and beyond," SFGate, February 23, 2024. https:// www.sfgate.com/la/article/in-n-out-drive-thru-two-way-speaker-harry-snyder-18678273.php.

24. McDowell, Erin. "How In-N-Out Invented the 2-way Speaker System and Created the First Modern Drive-thru." *Business Insider*, April 20, 2023. https://www.businessinsider.com/in-n-out-burger-first-drive-thru-history.

25. Calderone, Ana. "Who Is Lynsi Snyder? 5 Fascinating Facts About the Reclusive Heiress Who Owns In-N-Out Burger." *People.Com*, May 15, 2017. https://people.com/food/lynsi-snyder-in-n-out-billionaire-heir ess/.

26. Murray, Jeff. "The bias toward complexity when humans attempt to solve problems," Fordham Institute Flypaper, April 29, 2021. https:// fordhaminstitute.org/national/commentary/bias-toward-complexity-when-humans-attempt-solve-problems.

27. Adams, Gabrielle S., Benjamin A. Converse, Andrew H. Hales, and Leidy E. Klotz. "People Systematically Overlook Subtractive Changes." *Nature* 592, no. 7853 (2021): 258–61. https://www.nature.com/articles/s41586-021-03380-y#citeas.

28. Koski, Jessica E., Xie Hongling, and Ingrid R. Olson. "Understanding Social Hierarchies: The Neural and Psychological Foundations of Status Perception." *Social Neuroscience* 10, no. 5 (2015): 527–50. https:// pmc.ncbi.nlm.nih.gov/articles/PMC5494206/.

29. University of Waterloo. "Simplicity Is Key: Study Finds Our Minds Favor Simple Explanations and Efficient Actions." *MedicalXpress*, November 22, 2024. https://medicalxpress.com/news/2024-11-simplic ity-key-minds-favor-simple.html.

30. Lukas, Bryan. "Building a Winning Market Strategy: The Importance of Simplicity, Focus, and Routine," August 8, 2023. http://www.alliancembs .manchester.ac.uk/original-thinking-applied/original-thinkers/building-a-winning-market-strategy-the-importance-of-simplicity-focus-and-rou tine/.

31. Schwarz, Jeff, Indranil Roy, Maren Hauptmann, Yves Van Durme, and Brad Denny. "Leadership for the 21st Century: The Intersection of the Traditional and the New," Deloitte Insights, April 11, 2019. https:// www2.deloitte.com/us/en/insights/focus/human-capital-trends/2019/ 21st-century-leadership-challenges-and-development.html.

32. Sander, Elizabeth (Libby), Arran Caza, and Peter J. Jordan. "Psychological perceptions matter: Developing the reactions to the physical work environment scale," Building and Environment 148, January 15, 2019. https://www.sciencedirect.com/science/article/abs/pii/S03601323 18307157.

33. Roster, Catherine A., and Joseph R. Ferrari. "Does Work Stress Lead to Office Clutter, and How? Mediating Influences of Emotional Exhaustion and Indecision." *Environment and Behavior* 52, no. 9 (2019): 923–44. https://journals.sagepub.com/doi/abs/10.1177/0013916518823041? journalCode=eaba.

34. Mateo, Ricardo, José Roberto Hernández, Carmen Jaca, and Szabolcs Blazek. "Effects of tidy/messy work environment on human accuracy," *Management Decision* 51, November 2013. https://www.researchgate.net/ publication/260208727_Effects_of_tidymessy_work_environment_on_ human_accuracy.

35. Bellezza, Silvia, Neeru Paharia, and Anat Keinan. "Conspicuous Consumption of Time: When Busyness and Lack of Leisure Time Become a Status Symbol." *Journal of Consumer Research* 44, no. 1 (2016): 118–38. https://academic.oup.com/jcr/article-abstract/44/1/118/2736404?.

36. Laker, Benjamin, Vijay Pereira, Ashish Malik, and Lebene Soga. "Dear Manager, You're Holding Too Many Meetings." *Harvard Business Review*, March 9, 2022. https://hbr.org/2022/03/dear-manager-youre-holding-too-many-meetings.

Chapter 6

1. Paul, Karsten and Alfons Hollederer, "Unemployment and Job Search Behavior Among People With Disabilities During the First Year of the COVID-19 Pandemic in Germany," *International Journal of Environmental Research and Public Health* 20, no. 11 (2023): 6036. https:// pmc.ncbi.nlm.nih.gov/articles/PMC10252648.

2. Bureau of Labor Statistics. "Persons With a Disability: Labor Force Characteristics - 2024 A01 Results," February 25, 2025. https://www.bls.gov/news.release/disabl.toc.htm.
3. Ives-Rublee, Mia, Rose Khattar, and Lily Roberts. "Removing Obstacles for Disabled Workers Would Strengthen the U.S. Labor Market," American Progress, May 24, 2022. https://www.americanprogress.org/article/removing-obstacles-for-disabled-workers-would-strengthen-the-u-s-labor-market.
4. Ananian, Sevane, and Giulia Dellaferrera. "A Study on the Employment and Wage Outcomes of People With Disabilities," International Labour Organization, August 27, 2024. https://www.ilo.org/publications/study-employment-and-wage-outcomes-people-disabilities.
5. Pagano, Angelina C. "The Issue of Unemployment Among People with Disabilities," English Department Research for Change - Wicked Problems in Our World 70, April 8, 2021. https://research.library.kutztown.edu/cgi/viewcontent.cgi?article=1051&context=wickedproblems.
6. O'Dwyer, Maire, Philip McCallion, Mary McCarron, and Martin Henman. "Medication Use and Potentially Inappropriate Prescribing in Older Adults With Intellectual Disabilities: A Neglected Area of Research." *Therapeutic Advances in Drug Safety* 9, no. 9 (2018): 535–57. https://pmc.ncbi.nlm.nih.gov/articles/PMC6116771.
7. Visser, Casandra. "Grants for People With Disabilities (Updated in 2024)." *Accessibility Checker*, May 12, 2025. https://www.accessibilitychecker.org/blog/grants-for-people-with-disabilities/#.
8. Nagle, James J. "Trading Stamps: A Long History," *The New York Times*, December 26, 1971. https://www.nytimes.com/1971/12/26/archives/trading-stamps-a-long-history-premiums-said-to-date-back-in-us-to.html.
9. Chapple, Lidiya, Clay Cowan, Ellen Scully, and Jillian Tellez Holub. "Travel Invented Loyalty as We Know It. Now It's Time for Reinvention." *McKinsey & Company*, November 15, 2023. https://www.mckinsey.com/industries/travel-logistics-and-infrastructure/our-insights/travel-invented-loyalty-as-we-know-it-now-its-time-for-reinvention.
10. Santo, Brian. "The Consumer Electronics Hall of Fame: Atari 2600." *IEEE Spectrum*, November 22, 2022. https://spectrum.ieee.org/the-consumer-electronics-hall-of-fame-atari-2600.
11. Centre for Computing History. "Carol Shaw," n.d. https://www.computinghistory.org.uk/det/47370/Carol-Shaw.
12. Legaki, Nikoletta-Zampeta, Nannan Xi, Juho Hamari, Kostas Karpouzis, and Vassilios Assimakopoulos. "The effect of challenge-based gamification on learning: An experiment in the context of statistics education," *International Journal of Human-Computer Studies* 144, December 2020.

https://www.sciencedirect.com/science/article/pii/S1071581920300987?
via%3Dihub.

13. American Chemical Society. "High Performance Carbon Fibers,"
National Historic Chemical Landmarks Program, September 17, 2003.
https://www.acs.org/education/whatischemistry/landmarks/carbon
fibers.html.

14. Jenkins, Dennis R. "The Shuttle's Thermal Protection System (TPS),"
NASA History, April 5, 2001. https://www.nasa.gov/history/sts1/
pages/tps.html.

15. Schrauf, R. and Sanchez, J. "The Preponderance of Negative Emotion Words in the Emotion Lexicon: A Cross-generational and Cross-
linguistic Study." *Journal of Multilingual and Multicultural Development.*
25, no. 2–3 (2004): 266–84.

16. Sullivan, S., Mikels, J., Carstensen, L. "You Never Lose the Ages You've
Been: Affective Perspective Taking in Older Adults." *APA PsycNet.* 25, no.
1 (2010): 229.

17. Ritter, A., Franz, M., Miltner, W., and Weiss, T. *How Words Impact on
Pain.* NIH National Library of Medicine and the National Center for
Biotechnology Information, 2019.

18. Wroblewski, M.T. "Examples of positive communication in the workplace," Chron.com, n.d. https://smallbusiness.chron.com/examples-posi
tive-communication-workplace-11032.html.

19. Oldham, G. and Cummings, A. Employee Creativity Personal and
Contextual Factors at Work. *Academy of Management Journal.* 39, no. 3
(1996): 607–34.

20. Muniz-Velazquez, J. and Pulido, C. (2019). *The Routledge Handbook of Positive Communication Contributions of an Emerging Community of Research on
Communication for Happiness and Social Change.* Taylor & Francis. Chapters 2, 3 and 6.

21. Meyer, M. and Huhn, M. "Positive Language and Virtuous Leadership:
Walking the Talk." *Management Research* 18, no. 3 (2020): 263–84.

22. Mayfield, J. and Mayfield, M. *Motivating Language Theory: Effective
Leader Talk in the Workplace* (Palgrave Macmillan: 2018).

23. Zabelina, Darya L., Daniel O'Leary, Narun Pornpattananangkul, Robin
Nusslock, and Mark Beeman. "Creativity and Sensory Gating Indexed by
the P50: Selective Versus Leaky Sensory Gating in Divergent Thinkers
and Creative Achievers." *Neuropsychologia Journal* 69 (2015): 77–84.

24. Lee, Sang Won, Hyunsil Cha, Tae Yang Jang, Eunji Kim, Huijin Song,
Yongmin Chang, and Seung Jae Lee. "The Neural Correlates of Posi-
tive Versus Negative Thought-action Fusion in Healthy Young Adults."
Clinical Psychopharmacology and Neuroscience. 19, no. 4 (2021): 628.

25. Harvard Medical School and Massachusetts General Hospital. "Harvard Study of Adult Development," n.d. https://www.adultdevelop mentstudy.org.

Chapter 7

1. Florida State Parks. "Battle of Olustee Reenactment," n.d. https://www.floridastateparks.org/learn/battle-olustee-reenactment.
2. Wynne, Lewis N. and Robert A. Taylor. *Florida In The Civil War*. Arcadia Publishing, 2001.
3. Combined Books, ed. (2008). *The Civil War Book of Lists*. Book Sales, Inc. p. 97. ISBN 978-0-7858-1702-4.
4. Fasulo, Thomas R. "Battle of Olustee" n.d. https://web.archive.org/web/20080917234612/http://battleofolustee.org/.
5. Florida State Parks. "History of Olustee," n.d. https://www.floridastate parks.org/learn/history-olustee.
6. Essential Civil War Curriculum. "Civil War Reenacting - Essential Civil War Curriculum," n.d. https://www.essentialcivilwarcurriculum.com/civil-war-reenacting.html.
7. Bock, Jon and John Banks. "Cannon Fire and Cotton Candy: The 125th Anniversary Reenactment of Gettysburg." HistoryNet, May 11, 2023. https://www.historynet.com/largest-civil-war-reenactment-gettys burg/.
8. Farhi, Paul. "Civil War Reenactment Etiquette: How – and When – to Die on the Battlefield." *The Washington Post*, May 20, 2023. https://www.washingtonpost.com/lifestyle/style/civil-war-reenactment-eti quette-how--and-when--to-die-on-the-battlefield/2011/07/11/gIQAg NcRGI_story.html.
9. Matloob, Hasnain. "Touching the Void: Blurring Lines in Historical Reenactment | 2024 Review." *Factual America* Podcast, August 31, 2024. https://www.factualamerica.com/documentary-dilemmas/touching-the-void-documentary-blurs-lines-between-reenactment-and-reconstruction.
10. Kennedy, Barbara Noe. "Life of a Civil War Reenactor." Blue and Gray Education Society, October 29, 2019. https://blueandgrayeducation.org/2019/10/life-of-a-civil-war-reenactor/.
11. Daily Press. "CIVIL WAR RE-ENACTORS: 'WE'RE JUST LIVING HISTORY'" *Daily Press*, July 29, 2019. https://www.dailypress.com/2008/04/04/civil-war-re-enactors-were-just-living-history/.
12. U.S. National Park Service. "Hardtack During the Civil War," Manassas National Battlefield Park website, n.d. https://www.nps.gov/mana/learn/kidsyouth/hardtack-during-the-civil-war.htm.
13. "Battle of Olustee Reenactment Schedule Information," n.d. https://bat tleofolustee.org/forms_docs/schedule.html.

14. Moore, Nathaniel. "Civil War Reenactors Aren't Just Play-Acting. They Expect a War." *The New Republic*, October 21, 2024. https://newrepublic.com/article/185053/civil-war-reenactors-virginia-play-acting-expect-war.

15. Tanzi, Vito. "Corruption Around the World: Causes, Consequences, Scope, and Cures," Working Paper of the International Monetary Fund, May 1998. https://www.imf.org/external/pubs/ft/wp/wp9863.pdf.

16. Acres, Tom. "Fake AI images keep going viral," Sky News, December 13, 2023. https://news.sky.com/story/fake-ai-images-keep-going-viral-here-are-eight-that-have-caught-people-out-13028547.

17. AFP Staff Writer. "Fake AI History Photos Cloud the Past." The Globe Post, October 16, 2024. https://theglobepost.com/2024/10/16/fake-ai-history-photos/.

18. Xiang, Chloe. "People Are Creating Records of Fake Historical Events Using AI." *VICE*, July 27, 2024. https://www.vice.com/en/article/people-are-creating-records-of-fake-historical-events-using-ai/.

19. Designboom. "From 'Puffy Pope' to Trump's Arrest & Russia's Blue Plague, Fake AI Images Are Going Viral." *Designboom | Architecture & Design Magazine*, August 21, 2023. https://www.designboom.com/technology/puffy-pope-trump-arrest-blue-plague-fake-ai-03-29-2023/.

20. Da Silva Ehalt, Rômulo. "The Specter of AI-Generated Historical Documents," Legal History Insights, May 2, 2024. https://legalhistoryinsights.com/the-specter-of-ai-generated-historical-documents/.

21. Bordoloi, Satyen K. "The Hilarious & Horrifying Hallucinations of AI." Sify, February 8, 2023. https://www.sify.com/ai-analytics/the-hilarious-and-horrifying-hallucinations-of-ai/.

22. Hersh. "Has Social Media Made Us Stupid?" *Aish.com*, December 16, 2024. https://aish.com/has-social-media-made-our-country-stupid/.

23. USCIS. "Civics (History and Government) Questions for the Naturalization Test," 2019. https://www.uscis.gov/sites/default/files/document/questions-and-answers/100q.pdf.

24. Institute for Citizens & Scholars. "National Survey Finds Just 1 in 3 Americans Would Pass Citizenship Test," October 31, 2022. https://citizensandscholars.org/resource/national-survey-finds-just-1-in-3-americans-would-pass-citizenship-test/.

25. National Constitution Center "The Day the Constitution Was Ratified," June 21, 2024. https://constitutioncenter.org/blog/the-day-the-constitution-was-ratified.

26. Cheng, Isabella. "Can you pass the U.S. Citizenship Test?" KTAL News, February 3, 2024. https://www.ktalnews.com/news/us-politics/can-you-pass-the-u-s-citizenship-test/.

27. Dore, Kate. "Powerball Jackpot Hits $543 Million. What's the Best Payout Option? Experts Weigh Lump Sum Vs. Annuity." *CNBC*, December 19, 2023. https://www.cnbc.com/2023/12/18/powerball-jackpot-lump-sum-vs-annuity-which-option-is-better.html.

28. ABC News. "Three Powerball Winners Come Forward," August 27, 2001. https://abcnews.go.com/US/story?id=92592&page=1.

29. Joseph, Chris. "David Lee Edwards, Powerball Winner, Dies Broke in Hospice." New Times Broward-Palm Beach, December 5, 2013. https://www.browardpalmbeach.com/news/david-lee-edwards-powerball-winner-dies-broke-in-hospice-6470093.

30. Roback, Jennifer. "Who Was David Lee Edwards and What Happened to Him?." *The US Sun*, May 2, 2023. https://www.the-sun.com/news/8019584/who-david-lee-edwards-taylor-what-happened-lottery/.

31. Next Gen Personal Finance "What Percent of Lottery Winners Eventually Go Bankrupt?" NGPF, January 18, 2023. https://www.ngpf.org/blog/question-of-the-day/question-of-the-day-what-percent-of-lottery-winners-eventually-go-bankrupt/.

32. Acar, Oguz A., Murat Tarakci, and Daan Van Knippenberg. "Creativity and Innovation Under Constraints: A Cross-Disciplinary Integrative Review." *Journal of Management* 45, no. 1 (2018): 96–121. https://journals.sagepub.com/doi/10.1177/0149206318805832.

33. Moore, Susan. "Innovate in a Resource-Constrained Environment," Gartner, October 29, 2019. https://www.gartner.com/smarterwithgartner/innovate-resource-constrained-environment.

34. https://www.sciencedirect.com/science/article/abs/pii/S1057740814000916?np=y.

35. Iyengar, Sheena S., and Mark R. Lepper. "When Choice Is Demotivating: Can One Desire Too Much of a Good Thing?" *Journal of Personality and Social Psychology* 79, no. 6 (2000): 995–1006. https://pubmed.ncbi.nlm.nih.gov/11138768/.

36. Reuters. "Special Report: How Caterpillar got bulldozed in China," January 22, 2014. https://www.reuters.com/article/business/energy/special-report-how-caterpillar-got-bulldozed-in-china-idUSL3N0IT1SV/.

37. Global M&A Network, "Congratulations 2012 Winners Circle," The M&A Atlas Awards, November 18, 2012. https://globalmanetwork.com/2019/wp-content/uploads/2018/12/2012-Asia-Pacific-MA-Atlas-Awards-Winners-Circle.pdf.

38. Hawksford. "Chinese Accounting vs. International Financial Reporting Standards: What Are the Main Differences?"April 8, 2020. https://www.hawksford.com/insights-and-guides/china-business-guides/chinese-accounting-standards-vs-ifrs.

39. Gamse, Joe. "Top 13 Worst Mergers in History and Why They Failed." Ideals VDR Blog, 29 April 2025. https://www.idealsvdr.com/blog/worst-mergers-and-acquisitions-in-history-of-data-rooms/.

Chapter 8

1. Auchmutey, Jim. "From Lawless to Lawyer," *Atlanta Journal-Constitution*, October 25, 2015. https://specials.myajc.com/lawless-to-lawyer/.
2. Resney, Alex. "Mass Incarceration in the United States - Ballard Brief." *Ballard Brief*, October 16, 2024. https://ballardbrief.byu.edu/issue-briefs/mass-incarceration-in-the-united-states.
3. The Sentencing Project. "Mass Incarceration Trends," May 31, 2024. https://www.sentencingproject.org/reports/mass-incarceration-trends/.
4. Rovner, Joshua. "Youth Justice by the Numbers." The Sentencing Project, November 15, 2024. https://www.sentencingproject.org/policy-brief/youth-justice-by-the-numbers/.
5. "Justice Department Releases Ten-Year Recidivism Study | Prison Legal News," March 1, 2022. https://www.prisonlegalnews.org/news/2022/mar/1/justice-department-releases-ten-year-recidivism-study/.
6. Red. "Tackling Recidivism Through Education and Support." *RED - Stop Recidivism*, November 28, 2023. https://stoprecidivism.org/recidivism/tackling-recidivism-through-education-and-support/.
7. HISTORY.com Editors. "Daimler-Benz Announces Purchase of Chrysler Corp." HISTORY, May 27, 2025. https://www.history.com/this-day-in-history/daimler-benz-announces-purchase-of-chrysler-corp.
8. Evie, Lilly, and Ashley Dugger. "History of Prisons: Overview & Purpose." Study.com, November 21, 2023. https://study.com/learn/lesson/prisons-history-characteristics-purpose.html.
9. Halley, Catherine. "The Invention of Incarceration." *JSTOR Daily*, November 11, 2024. https://daily.jstor.org/the-invention-of-incarceration/.
10. Hirst, J. "Australian Experience: The Convict Colony| Office of Justice Programs," 1995. https://www.ojp.gov/ncjrs/virtual-library/abstracts/australian-experience-convict-colony-oxford-history-prison-practice.
11. Bleicher, Ariel. "Norway's Humane Approach to Prisons Can Work Here Too." *UCSF Magazine*, Summer 2021. https://magazine.ucsf.edu/norways-humane-approach-prisons-can-work-here-too.
12. Alliance, First Step. "Rehabilitation Lessons From Norway's Prison System." First Step Alliance (blog), May 2, 2024. https://www.firststepalliance.org/post/norway-prison-system-lessons.
13. Bleicher, Ariel. "Norway's Humane Approach to Prisons Can Work Here Too." *UCSF Magazine*, Summer 2021. https://magazine.ucsf.edu/norways-humane-approach-prisons-can-work-here-too.

14. Ekunwe, Ikponwosa O., Richard S. Jones, Kaley Mullin. "Public Attitudes Toward Crime and Incarceration in Finland," The Jackson State University Researcher 23(1), Spring 2010. https://epublications.marque tte.edu/cgi/viewcontent.cgi?article=1157&context=socs_fac.
15. Sørensen, K. M., G. Midtlyng, and O.C.Boe. "Educating for a Better Understanding of Dynamic Security in a Prison Context: How Prison Officers can Learn to Better Read and Calibrate Their Responses to Violent Inmates," *ICERI2024 Proceedings*, 2024, pp. 2291–99.
16. Djordejevic, Patrick. "What we know about El Salvador's megaprison," NewsNation, March 17, 2025. https://www.newsnationnow.com/crime/what-we-know-el-salvador-megaprison/.
17. Benko, Jessica. "The Radical Humaneness of Norway's Halden Prison," *New York Times*, March 26, 2015. https://www.nytimes.com/2015/03/29/magazine/the-radical-humaneness-of-norways-halden-prison.html.
18. O'Neill Heather. "The Road Not Taken: Greatest Career Regrets Revealed." *Resume-Now*, January 8, 2025. https://www.resume-now.com/job-resources/careers/career-regrets.
19. Clifford, Cat. "New Research Busts the Myth of the 20-something Start-up Founder." *CNBC*, December 8, 2016. https://www.cnbc.com/2016/12/08/new-research-busts-the-myth-of-the-20-something-start-up-founder.html.
20. Hendry, Erica R. "7 Epic Fails Brought to You by the Genius Mind of Thomas Edison." *Smithsonian Magazine*, December 4, 2013. https://www.smithsonianmag.com/innovation/7-epic-fails-brought-to-you-by-the-genius-mind-of-thomas-edison-180947786/.
21. Grothaus, Michael. "'Angry Birds' Maker Rovio's Bold Plan to Slingshot Its Way To Future Growth," *Fast Company*, March 21, 2015. https://www.fastcompany.com/3043466/ceo-pekka-rantala-insists-rovio-maker-of-angry-birds-can-slingshot-its-way-to-disney-sized-g.
22. Warner, Eric. "Angry Birds' Impact on Mobile Gaming Is Still Felt 15 Years Later." *Game Rant*, December 11, 2024. https://gamer ant.com/angry-birds-15-year-anniversary-mobile-gaming-impact/.

Chapter 9

1. Roser, Max and Hannah Ritchie. "How Has World Population Growth Changed Over Time?" *Our World in Data*, June 1, 2023. https://our worldindata.org/population-growth-over-time.
2. Robert Zubrin. "The Population Control Holocaust," The New Atlantis, Spring 2012. https://www.thenewatlantis.com/publications/the-popula tion-control-holocaust.

3. The Economist. "Global Fertility Has Collapsed, With Profound Economic Consequences." *The Economist*, June 1, 2023. https://www.economist.com/leaders/2023/06/01/global-fertility-has-collapsed-with-profound-economic-consequences.

4. Institute for Health Metrics and Evaluation. "The Lancet: Dramatic Declines in Global Fertility Rates Set to Transform Global Population Patterns by 2100," March 20, 2024. https://www.healthdata.org/news-events/news room/news-releases/lancet-dramatic-declines-global-fertility-rates-set-transform.

5. Madgavkar, Anu, Marc Canal Noguer, Chris Bradley, Olivia White, Sven Smit, and Radigan, T. J. "Dependency and Depopulation? Confronting the Consequences of a New Demographic Reality." *McKinsey & Company*, January 15, 2025. https://www.mckinsey.com/mgi/our-research/depend ency-and-depopulation-confronting-the-consequences-of-a-new-demo graphic-reality.

6. Cylus, J. and Al Tayara, L. "Health, an Ageing Labour Force, and the Economy: Does Health Moderate the Relationship Between Population Age-Structure and Economic Growth?" *Social Science & Medicine* 287, 2021: 114353. https://doi.org/10.1016/j.socscimed.2021.114353.

7. Locke, John. "Two Treatises of Government." Uploaded by Rod Hay. London: Printed for Thomas Tegg; W. Sharpe and Son; G. Offor; G. and J. Robinson; J. Evans and Co.: Also R. Griffin and Co. Glasgow; and J. Gumming, Dublin, 1823. https://www.yorku.ca/comninel/courses/3025pdf/Locke.pdf.

8. McCrum, Robert. "The 100 Best Nonfiction Books: No. 87 - a Treatise of Human Nature by David Hume (1739)." *The Guardian*, October 2, 2017. https://www.theguardian.com/books/2017/oct/02/david-hume-treatise-human-nature-nonfiction-robert-mccrum-100-best.

9. Tun, Zaw Thiha. "Theranos: A Fallen Unicorn." *Investopedia*, March 21, 2025. https://www.investopedia.com/articles/investing/020116/theranos-fallen-unicorn.asp.

10. Crockett, Zachary. "The rise and demise of the AAirpass, American Airlines' $250k lifetime ticket." *The Hustle*, April 7, 2018. https://the hustle.co/aairpass-american-airlines-250k-lifetime-ticket.

11. Rothstein, Caroline. "My Father Had a Lifelong Ticket to Fly Anywhere. Then They Took It Away." *The Guardian*, September 20, 2019. https://www.theguardian.com/lifeandstyle/2019/sep/19/american-airlines-aair pass-golden-ticket.

12. Bensinger, Ken. "The Frequent Fliers Who Flew Too Much." *Los Angeles Times*, May 5, 2012. https://www.latimes.com/travel/la-xpm-2012-may-05-la-fi-0506-golden-ticket-20120506-story.html.

13. Pennock, Lewis. "Inside American Airlines' $250,000 Lifetime Pass: How ticket that granted unlimited first class flights became a DISASTER for airline, after customers, including Mark Cuban took thousands of trips and cost company millions." *Daily Mail*, July 1, 2023. https://www.dailymail.co.uk/news/article-12240265/Inside-American-Airlines-250k-lifetime-pass-grants-unlimited-class-travel.html.

14. Bensinger, Ken. "The Frequent Fliers Who Flew Too Much," *Los Angeles Times*, May 5, 2012. https://www.latimes.com/travel/la-xpm-2012-may-05-la-fi-0506-golden-ticket-20120506-story.html.

15. Peters, Luke. "How One Man Cost American Airlines £21M Using His Lifetime First Class Air Pass." *AeroTime*, February 10, 2025. https://www.aerotime.aero/articles/american-airlines-unlimited-airpass-story-steven-rothstein.

16. Madison, Ivory. "Why Your Social Media Metrics Are a Waste of Time." *Harvard Business Review*, December 18, 2012. https://hbr.org/2012/12/why-your-social-media-metrics.

17. Lord, Christopher. "Rush's Geddy Lee: 'Punk Bands Made Us Seem Like Beethoven by Comparison'." *The Guardian*, November 16, 2023. https://www.theguardian.com/culture/2023/nov/16/rush-geddy-lee-reader-interview.

18. PBS. "Frederick W. Smith," Who Made America?, n.d. https://www.pbs.org/wgbh/theymadeamerica/whomade/fsmith_hi.html.

19. Martin, David. "FedEx: A 50-year Revolution of Business." *CBS News*, June 4, 2023. https://www.cbsnews.com/news/federal-express-fred-smith-50-years-of-fedex/.

20. We Are Memphis. "FedEx Named One of the World's Most Admired Companies for 25th Consecutive Year," January 30, 2025. https://wearememphis.com/news/fedex-named-one-of-the-worlds-most-admired-companies-for-25th-consecutive-year.

21. Walshe, Sadhbh. "Is Fast Food With Integrity Possible?" *The Guardian*, March 1, 2013. https://www.theguardian.com/sustainable-business/chipotle-fast-food-integrity.

22. Tyler. "How Chipotle Revolutionized Fast Food," Harvard Technology and Operations Management, MBA Student Perspectives, December 9, 2015. https://d3.harvard.edu/platform-rctom/submission/how-chipotle-revolutionized-fast-food/.

23. McFarland, Matt. "Segway was supposed to change the world. Two decades later, it just might," CNN.com, October 30, 2018. https://www.cnn.com/2018/10/30/tech/segway-history/index.html.

24. Davies, Chris. "Self-Balancing Butt of a Thousand Jokes, the Segway Is Being Discontinued." *SlashGear*, June 23, 2020. https://www.slashgear.com/self-balancing-butt-of-a-thousand-jokes-the-segway-is-being-discontinued-23626125/.

Chapter 10

1. Gillis, Kaytee. "Why Am I So Unhappy? 15 Explanations From a Therapist," ChoosingTherapy.com, June 4. 2025. https://www.choosingther apy.com/why-am-i-so-unhappy/.

2. Festinger, Leon. "A Theory of Social Comparison Processes." *Human Relations* 7, no. 2 (May 1, 1954): 117–40. https://doi.org/10.1177/001872675400700202.

3. Fandom. "1955 in television," n.d. https://americantvdatabase.fan dom.com/wiki/Category:1955_in_television.

4. Samra, Adele, Wayne A. Warburton, and Andrew M. Collins. "Social Comparisons: A Potential Mechanism Linking Problematic Social Media Use With Depression." *Journal of Behavioral Addictions* 11, no. 2 (June 2, 2022): 607–14. https://pmc.ncbi.nlm.nih.gov/articles/PMC9295248/.

5. Lin, Liu Yi, Jaime E. Sidani, Ariel Shensa, Ana Radovic, Elizabeth Miller, Jason B. Colditz, Beth L. Hoffman, Leila M. Giles, and Brian A. Primack. "Association Between Social Media Use and Depression Among U.S. Young Adults." *Depression and Anxiety* 33, no. 4 (January 19, 2016): 323–31. https://pubmed.ncbi.nlm.nih.gov/26783723/.

6. Hussain, Zaheer and Mark D. Griffiths. "Problematic Social Networking Site Use and Comorbid Psychiatric Disorders: A Systematic Review of Recent Large-Scale Studies." *Frontiers in Psychiatry* 9 (December 14, 2018). https://www.frontiersin.org/journals/psychiatry/articles/10.3389/fpsyt.2018.00686/full.

7. Durak, Hatice Yıldız. "Modeling of Variables Related to Problematic Internet Usage and Problematic Social Media Usage in Adolescents." *Current Psychology* 39, no. 4 (April 3, 2018): 1375–87. https://link.springer.com/article/10.1007/s12144-018-9840-8.

8. Pellegrino, Alfonso, Alessandro Stasi, and Veera Bhatiasevi. "Research Trends in Social Media Addiction and Problematic Social Media Use: A Bibliometric Analysis." *Frontiers in Psychiatry* 13 (November 10, 2022). https://www.frontiersin.org/journals/psychiatry/articles/10.3389/fpsyt.2022.1017506/full.

9. Wadmin. "The Psychology of Comparison: Why We Do It and How to Stop Now and in the Future." Mindful Health Solutions, November 3, 2023. https://mindfulhealthsolutions.com/the-psychology-of-compari son-why-we-do-it-and-how-to-stop/.

10. American Museum of Natural History. "Creativity and Community: How Modern Humans Overcame the Neanderthals," ScienceDaily, April 21, 2021. https://www.sciencedaily.com/releases/2021/04/210421100932.htm.

11. Oppert, Michelle Leanne, Valerie O'Keefe, Markus Søbstad Bensnes, Alin L. Grecu, David H. Cropley. "The value of creativity: A scoping review," *Journal of Creativity*, 33(2), August 2023. https://www.sciencedirect.com/science/article/pii/S2713374523000183.

12. World Economic Forum. "Future of Jobs Report 2023," May 2023. https://www3.weforum.org/docs/WEF_Future_of_Jobs_2023.pdf.

13. Canva and Harvard Business Review Analytic Services. "Creativity as a Catalyst for Business Growth," Harvard Business School Publishing, 2024. https://www.canva.com/resources/creativity-for-business-growth-report.

14. Koivisto, M. and Grassini, S. "Best Humans Still Outperform Artificial Intelligence in a Creative Divergent Thinking Task." *Scientific Reports* 13, 13601 (2023). https://doi.org/10.1038/s41598-023-40858-3.

15. Mcalister, Sean. "From Jesse Owens to Usain Bolt: The evolution of the men's 100m world record." Olympics.Com, July 14, 2022. https://www.olympics.com/en/news/jesse-owens-usain-bolt-evolution-100m-world-record.

16. USA Track & Field. "Ralph Craig," n.d. https://www.usatf.org/athlete-bios/ralph-craig.

17. Statathlon. "Historical & Predictive Analysis for the 100m Sprint Race." n.d. https://statathlon.com/historical-predictive-analysis-for-the-100m-sprint-race/.

18. World Athletics. "100 Metres Men: 12th IAAF World Championships in Athletics. n.d. https://worldathletics.org/results/iaaf-world-championships-in-athletics/2009/12th-iaaf-world-championships-in-athletics-6998524/men/100-metres/final/result.

19. Radico, Julie. "Stop Comparing Yourself Negatively to Others," *Psychology Today*, April 22, 2024. https://www.psychologytoday.com/us/blog/you-are-enough/202404/stop-comparing-yourself-negatively-to-others.

20. CNN Money. "After a painful bankruptcy she created a multimillion dollar marketing firm," WGNO, August 19, 2016. https://wgno.com/news/after-a-painful-bankruptcy-she-created-a-multi-million-dollar-marketing-firm.

21. Beard, Alison. "Life's Work: An Interview With Vera Wang." *Harvard Business Review*, July/August 2019. https://hbr.org/2019/07/lifes-work-an-interview-with-vera-wang.

22. Shulman, Sophie. "A Diamond in the Rough: The Story of SimilarWeb Founder or Offer." CTech by Calcalist, August 15, 2021. https://www.calcalistech.com/ctech/articles/0,7340,L-3915232,00.html.

23. Cicero, M.T. (2012) *On Living and Dying Well*. Penguin Books.

24. FastWill Staff Writer. "Which Billionaires Are Disinheriting Their Children?" FastWill n.d. https://fastwill.com/estate-planning-guide/news/these-billionaires-are-disinheriting-their-children/.

25. Chen, Ludwig C. H. "Knowledge of Beauty in Plato's Symposium." *The Classical Quarterly*. 33, no. 1 (1983): 66–74. Cambridge University. https://web.stanford.edu/~mvr2j/ucsccourse/BeautyinSymposium.pdf.

26. Foley, Devin. "10 Thought-Provoking Things Einstein Actually Said," Intellectual Takeout (blog), October 7, 2015. https://intellectualtakeout.org/2015/10/10-thought-provoking-things-einstein-actually-said/.

27. Roosevelt, Theodore. "The Strenuous Life," April 10, 1899. Available at: https://voicesofdemocracy.umd.edu/roosevelt-strenuous-life-1899-speech-text/.

28. Roosevelt, Theodore. "Address in Des Moines, Iowa," November 4, 1910. Available at: https://libquotes.com/theodore-roosevelt/quote/lbl2r7r.

Acknowledgments

This book would not have been possible without the love, support, energy, and great talent of someone I am lucky to call a friend: the brilliant editor Cheryl Segura. I cannot even begin to tell you how honored I am to have written two books together, and your continued guidance, sense of proportion, and literary brilliance is something I am deeply grateful for. Cheryl, you have always been someone I could rely on consistently over the years as a force of good in publishing with your fine sense of humor, passion, and belief in the transformative power of creativity. Shall we do another book together, Cheryl?

The world of modern publishing relies not only on great editors like Cheryl but also on great literary agents like Jessica Faust. Thank you, Jessica, for helping with all the contractual elements for this book. You and your team have been such a great resource over the years. Thank you for making the time to deal with all the ups and downs that come with having to represent authors like me. I am always grateful for your contributions and suggestions.

To the John Wiley & Sons team: Deb Schindlar, Amanda Pyne, Jeanenne Ray, Martin Tribe, Katie Helm, Shannon Vargo, and all the others who gave countless hours to this manuscript, my deepest appreciation. To Kelly Talbot for all the help making me look like a far better writer than I am, I thank you humbly, my good sir. Another warm thank you to Michele Matrisciani for being so amazing and awesome to work with and to Christina Verigan for catching things that slipped through the cracks. Also much appreciation and love to Donya Dickerson for helping me each step of the way.

To Titouan Bernicot, Catherine Plourde, and the rest of your team, thank you for offering help. I sure appreciate what you are doing in our oceans and outside of them, too. To Dr. Justin Valentin and Rosianna Jules, thank you for all you are doing in Seychelles with education. To Gil Winch, I supremely appreciate your sense of well-being and harmony, fairness, and balance in the world. You are making the world better every day through the use of commerce and employing people who were previously thought of as unemployable. Your work is a shining light of innovation and creativity and a worthwhile and noble undertaking. David Lee Windecher, you are an inspiration to all of us who have done wrong over the years. You have not only transformed yourself, but you are also now helping transform others, and the work you are doing is critical for the future of our great nation. I thank you sir for everything you have contributed to this book.

To Porsche Cars North America and AutoNation, a warm thank you goes out to Ben Ellis, Bryan Trejos, and Cleber Gomes Filho. To Rolex and Watches of Switzerland, another warm thank you to Carla Uzel, Krista Beyrer, Mark Goldberg, Jason Lopez, and the rest of the team for embracing this book and me so warmly, thoughtfully, and kindheartedly. I am so thankful not only for the fine timepieces you make which continue to drive emotional and poignant meaning for generations, but also for all the support throughout the years.

To my dear friend Kekai Beyer, thank you for listening to me go on and on about this book. Your contributions to this book have been lifelong and steadfast, and I admire you greatly. To my goddaughter Kailani, I cannot wait to see what light you continue to bestow upon the world around you and your community. Your gifts are multitudinous, and your brilliance radiant.

To my family: you are my everything. Jacob, you continue to be an inspiration to all around you and a bright light in our lives. I take great satisfaction in seeing you continue to provide good in the world. Your future is bright, and your wonderful spirit unmatched. Keep spreading light where there is darkness, hope where there is despair, and love where there is none.

About the Author

Nir Bashan is a leading authority on creativity in business, with a global track record of helping organizations drive performance, innovation, and growth through creative thinking. He is the founder of The Creator Mindset LLC, a consultancy that transforms how companies approach leadership, strategy, and problem-solving. Bashan has advised executives and front line teams at top-tier organizations including Porsche Cars North America, Dutch Bros Coffee, Thermo Fisher Scientific, and Cardinal Health. His work spans sectors such as healthcare, finance, manufacturing, and retail, where he delivers measurable results through practical, creative frameworks. He is the author of *The Creator Mindset*, named by Blinkist as a top 100 nonfiction book of all time, a widely adopted resource in corporate and academic settings, and a contributor to *Psychology Today*, where his articles have garnered millions of views globally. A sought-after keynote speaker, Bashan presents to audiences across the country and is regularly featured in outlets such as *Forbes*, *Fast Company*, NBC, NPR, and *Inc*.

Index